# PERMACULTURE DESIGN NOTES

EDITED BY DELVIN SOLKINSON
WITH KYM CHI

DESIGNED BY
ONBEYOND METAMEDIA

The companion to this book is the
*Permaculture Design Core Concepts Cards*
including principles, methods and strategies
not included in this volume.
**www.dewpermaculture.com**

Many other learning and teaching tools were
designed in conjunction with this book and
are used in our PDC practice.
**www.permaculturedesign.ca**

Copyright © 2017 by Permaculture Design

Attribution — Others must give appropriate credit, provide a link to the license, and indicate if changes were made. They may do so in any reasonable manner, but not in any way that suggests the licensor endorses you or your use. No additional restrictions — Others may not apply legal terms or technological measures that legally restrict others from doing anything the license permits.

Share Alike - Others may copy, distribute, display, perform, and modify this work, as long as they distribute any modified work on the same terms. If they want to distribute modified works under other terms, they must get your permission first.

Non Commercial - You let others copy, distribute, display, perform, and (unless you have chosen NoDerivatives) modify and use your work for any purpose other than commercially unless they get your permission first.

No Derivatives - You let others copy, distribute, display and perform only original copies of your work. If they want to modify your work, they must get your permission first.

First Printing: 2019
ISBN 978-1-7751148-2-6

Permaculture Design
1427 B Bonniebrook Heights Road
Gibsons, BC, V0N 1V5

www.permaculturedesign.ca


Ordering Information:
This book is available freely as a download at printable resolution
https://www.dewpermaculture.com/

The book is orderable through an on-demand printer with discounts for larger orders.
Note Lulu always has a sale on so make sure to find the discount code
http://www.lulu.com/shop/permaculture-design/

# PERMACULTURE DESIGN NOTES

EDITED BY DELVIN SOLKINSON
WITH KYM CHI

DESIGNED BY
ONBEYOND METAMEDIA

PERMACULTURE DESIGN 2017

# PRETRO
## INTENTIONS

Born from love and gratitude for this life, my work in permaculture is driven by an inspiration to be in service and give something back to help support others to Care for the Earth and its People.

At the time of publication of this new edition in 2017, I have spent 15 years travelling the planet to learn from many Pioneers of Permaculture by taking Permaculture Design Courses, Advanced Permaculture Programs and Teacher Trainings. From this experience I have taken notes on the core curriculum of the Permaculture Design Certificate Course.

Some students struggle to take notes and some teachers struggle to identify and deliver the core curriculum since the body of information in permaculture design is so vast. Using the teaching technique Larry Santoyo describes as 'Teaching by Overwhelm' does work to reprogram one's paradigm and upgrade their way of seeing the world. However, with no tests given in the permaculture design course, retention of specific information retention can be low.

The intention of this work is to support students and teachers alike by freely sharing this information with the World Community. It's my hope that this will be translated into many languages and be freely shared with people of all cultures across the planet.

These core curriculum notes can also be a design method, a driver for your design process. Read through them and see what you have incorporated already and what concepts may still inform your design. What strategies, techniques and attitudes can you incorporate into the design of your life, home, business, garden, or farm?

Missing from this work are most of the permaculture principles, strategies, attitudes and design methods, which can be found in the *Core Concepts Cards* at www.dewpermaculture.com

May any merit generated by this work be dedicated to the benefit of all beings.

Delvin Solkinson
email : delvin@cosm.org

Freely Available
**www.permaculturedesign.ca**

**PERMACULTURE WORKSHEET 000**

# PRETRO
## GRATITUDE

I have had amazing support from some of my closest co-teachers and permaculture allies to help refine, edit and expand these notes into a holistic Core Curriculum. This has truly become a group project.
I am so grateful to the human guild who collaborated on this with me. They have uplifted this far beyond what I could have ever done on my own.

I am profoundly grateful to to my co-teacher Kym Chi. She spent almost two years helping to read through, edit and playtest the Core Curriculum Notes over numerous PDC's. She has made many significant contributions throughout the text and structure of this work including a number of full worksheets including the *Design for Resilience* and *Medicine Making* sections.

Profound sacred gratitude to Annaliese Hordern who has been instrumental in this project on many levels. She sat next to me in many classes with permaculture elders and has contributed content and editing to this work.

Super thanks go to one of my permaculture heroes Tamara Griffiths who contributed in a foundational way to the first edition of the worksheets as well as proofing and editing recent editions.

Bows to Jacob Aman who has contributed in many ways to the life of this work including editing early editions.

Heartfelt gratitude to Unity Life Avatar who designed three template pages that housed the early editions of these worksheets for a decade. Her designs have uplifted and inspired this work on many levels.

Glowing thanks to Niki Hammond and Tes Tesla whose keen proofing helped address countless errors and typos that riddled the early editions.

Deep bows to Keala and La whose deep connected wisdom has helped inform and evolve this work on so many levels.

Freely Available
www.permaculturedesign.ca

PERMACULTURE WORKSHEET 000

# PRETRO
## GRATITUDE

The foundation of this work comes from my time spent over a 7 year span of time with Bill Mollison over a which included completing a PDC, Diploma and Masters Degree with him. He lifted me up and empowered my work on so many levels, placing me firmly on the permaculture path.

I want to recognize my primary mentors whose influence is at the very heart of this work as well as who contributed alot of the content in these Core Curriculum Notes. Deep low bows go to Larry Santoyo, my greatest hero and one of the most inspirational and masterful mentors and teachers I have studied with. Prostrations to the incredible visionary Looby Macnamara, a primary mentor who has taken this work to ever increasing evolutionary levels. Soul gratitude to Rosemary Morrow for helping me to refine the language of these notes and bringing the Ethics deeper into my life. She recognized my life mission to continuously advance my skills by completing advanced courses and teacher trainings to become the best mentor for graduates. So much thanks to Toby Hemenway whose inspiration rings through this work, his clear and accessible transmission of the science behind permaculture helped me to grasp it.

Deep acknowledgements to my other transformative teachers and mentors who have been instrumental in this work including being the source for much of this content. Low kowtows to Jason Gerhardt, a noble and dedicated permaculture monk. Kudos to Scott Pittman a worthy leader and guide for the movement. Respect goes to David Holmgren who taught me alot of foundational concepts and source information for this work. Props go to Geoff Lawton for bringing permaculture to many more people from all aspects of society and giving me a mission 'to make myself redundant'. Loving appreciation to Robin Clayfield who catalyzed my creativity and evolved my practice to include dynamic facilitation. Epic recognition to my hero Michael Becker whose mentorship has raised my permaculture practice into new possibilities and played a profound role in this work. Admiration to Starhawk who transformed the way I understand permaculture and dissolved the boundaries between the practice and a ritual life. Props to Doug and Sam Bullock whose classes at their exceptional food forest site was absolutely life changing. Loving thanks to Patricia Michael whose core influence can be seen and felt at the very heart of this work.

Freely Available
www.permaculturedesign.ca

# PRETRO
## GRATITUDE

This work would not be possible without advanced course transmissions from my other primary teachers. Epic thanks to one of my most beloved teachers, Mark Lakeman for bringing so much spirit to this movement and my own practice within it. The incredible information I learned from Tom Ward was life changing and continues to fill me with passion for permaculture. The amazing Jude Hobbs helped me understand the bridge between permaculture, gardening, landscaping and consulting and anchored me into the practice. I was humbled and empowered by the incredible Robyn Francis who brought me strongly into the reality of permaculture. Much love goes to Robina McCurdy whose passion and excitement for this work is contagious. Every blessing to Robin Wheeler, a master herbalist and profoundly important mentor in my life who co-taught the 144 hour PDC with me, half permaculture and half hands-on homesteading skills.

Special thanks to my dear mother who believed in and supported my path whole heartedly. More gratitude to my father who has been instrumental these past few years in helping me complete this work. I want to acknowledge Dana Wilson, the force behind much Gaiacraft media and all its photos and video, Karen Mckenzie who is a lantern in my life and for so many others in need, and my godparents Gabriel and Sapphire for their unconditional love and support through this whole process. Deepest thanks to the divine Grace for the love and adventures that gave me passion and inspiration to complete this work.

My dearest friend who has been designing my media since the mid-90's, continues to bring my work to the next level with his truly visionary design. Soul level gratitude to Sijay James **www.onbeyondmetamedia.com** the designer of this book, with its vectors and icons. His mastery is a profound blessing. Thanks to Shaun Friesen **www.freezen.ca** for his technical prowess in helping us dial the design for print. All my love goes to the countless teachers, friends and supporters who I have not mentioned in this all to lengthy introduction and apologies for not acknowledging you better.

This book is my way of giving back and supporting the evolution of the permaculture design movement. May it inspire and uplift your learning and teaching practice.

Delvin Solkinson, Winter Solstice 2017

Freely Available
www.permaculturedesign.ca

# PRETRO
## TABLE OF CONTENTS

| | | | | |
|---|---|---|---|---|
| **Introduction to Design** | | | **Design for Climate** | |
| Class Culture | 01 | | Energy Cycles | 80 |
| Reading the Designers Manual | 02 | | Microclimates | 83 |
| | | | Appropriate Technology | 86 |
| **Foundational Concepts** | | | | |
| Defining Permaculture | 04 | | **Design for Cool Climate** | |
| Ethos | 07 | | Seasonal Life | 92 |
| Key Characteristics | 09 | | | |
| Design Principles | 10 | | **Design for Tropics** | |
| | | | Abundant Life | 95 |
| **Design Methods** | | | | |
| Zones | 12 | | **Design for Drylands** | |
| Sectors | 19 | | Plant Life | 99 |
| Mapping Project | 12 | | Final Design Project | 106 |
| | | | | |
| **Pattern Literacy** | | | **Social Permaculture** | |
| World Code | 24 | | Governance | 108 |
| Guilds | 28 | | Organizational Structures | 112 |
| | | | Land for the Landless | 117 |
| **Soil** | | | Designers Checklist | 118 |
| Life Alchemy | 31 | | | |
| Composting | 32 | | **OS Permaculture** | |
| Soil Science | 43 | | Permanomics | 122 |
| | | | Placemaking | 127 |
| **Design for Trees** | | | Design for Resilience | 137 |
| Facts and Functions | 54 | | | |
| Food Micro-Forest Garden | 59 | | **Design Futures** | |
| | | | Post-PDC Permaculture | 144 |
| **Design for Animals** | | | Next Level Education | 148 |
| Integrative Farming | 65 | | | |
| Cool Climate Chicken Fodder | 68 | | **Medicine Making** | |
| Deep Ecology | 70 | | Wildcrafting Principles | 172 |
| | | | Harvesting Times | 174 |
| **Design for Water** | | | Herbal Classes | 175 |
| Life Source | 72 | | Preparations | 178 |
| Techniques | 75 | | Healing Plants | 185 |
| | | | Resources | 190 |

Freely Available
www.permaculturedesign.ca

# INTRODUCTION TO DESIGN
## CLASS CULTURE

**Creating Conscious Learning Environments**

- Remain Present
- Forgive yourself and each other
- Be kind, considerate and compassionate
- Make positive appreciative comments, never ridicule yourself or others ever
- Use hands signals when people are talking
- Speak up loudly so everyone can hear
- Use I statements and respectful language
- Be punctual
- Everyone has the right to speak and to pass on speaking
- Respect the airspace and just speak for yourself
- If you have a problem with someone, communicate with them directly
- Stick to the topic
- Accept that we are all at different places on our learning journey
- Co-operate not compete
- Shh - secrets stay here – confidentiality
- Honor disabilities and special needs
- Recognize we are all teachers and learners

**Source Curriculum :**
Rowe Morrow www.bluemountainspermacultureinstitute.com.au
Robin Clayfield www.dynamicgroups.com.au

**Envoy :** Delvin Solkinson www.visionarypermaculture.com

**Foundational Work :** Kym Chi www.gigglingchitree.com

**Gaiacraft Workbook Editing Team :** Delvin Solkinson, Kym Chi, Annaliese Hordern, Tamara Griffiths, Jacob Aman, Tes Tesla, Niki Hammond

**Design :** Sijay James www.onbeyondmetamedia.com

Freely Available
www.permaculturedesign.ca

**PERMACULTURE WORKSHEET 001**

# INTRODUCTION TO DESIGN
## READING THE DESIGNERS MANUAL

Spread out the readings! Don't try to do it all at once. Reading one chapter a month for 13 months at the pace of the class is a great way to do this. The book is modular so can be broken up easily into short reading periods.

Don't worry about memorizing the information. There are no tests. It's more about knowing where the information is than trying to take it all in, you may find that more of it sinks in than you might think.

Don't get caught up on stuff you don't understand, make a note of this and move on. Discussions about topics can happen later to gain clarity.

The designer manual is full of super dense information, a sentence is like a paragraph, a paragraph is like a chapter, and chapter is like a book.

Take notes or highlight! Some people retain more information if they do some creative note taking, underlining or highlighting the text.

Read with others! Buddy up for reading sessions to help motivate the reading.

Read it aloud! For some people this can can be done as a buddy system where things can be clarified through discussion.

Remember you never know where this information will take you. Pay attention to things even if they don't seem relevant in the moment. You may find yourself working, living or teaching in a different climate or on a huge farm one day!

The color photographic plates give great real world illustrations of the concepts being discussed.

Pay attention to the Designers Checklists at the back of each chapter. These are great reviews for the key points of each module.

Freely Available
www.permaculturedesign.ca

**PERMACULTURE WORKSHEET 002**

# INTRODUCTION TO DESIGN
## READING THE DESIGNERS MANUAL

For those who have the time to engage deeper into this learning process, Gaiacraft highly recommends reading 'Earth User's Guide to Permaculture' by Rosemary Morrow. You can read both books simultaneously and get a wise female perspective and writing style to mirror and compliment Bill Mollison's text.

Including a bioregionally specific permaculture text as well is another way to really bring this information home. Here in the temperate climates 'Gaia's Garden' by Toby Hemenway is often used. Having a couple books on the native plants and animals of your local bioregion as well as how they were used by First Peoples will also help round out your curriculum.

Combine the readings with observation walks around your home and community! Get out for nature walks. Integrative experiences where you can reflect on the materials can help you process and understand the information. Hands on learning with some of the techniques is also a wonderful way to learn this material and apply it directly to your life.

Most of all, have fun! See how you can creatively use your understanding of your own learning styles, ways of reading and approaches to text book work to help you get the most out of the process.

**Envoy :** Delvin Solkinson www.visionarypermaculture.com
**Foundational Work :** Kym Chi www.gigglingchitree.com
**Gaiacraft Workbook Editing Team :** Delvin Solkinson, Kym Chi, Annaliese Hordern, Tamara Griffiths, Jacob Aman, Tes Tesla, Niki Hammond
**Design :** Sijay James www.onbeyondmetamedia.com

Freely Available
www.permaculturedesign.ca

# FOUNDATIONAL CONCEPTS
## DEFINING PERMACULTURE

Permaculture is new speak, a conjunction of permanent and agriculture or culture. Here are some definitions of permaculture from the pioneers of the movement.

*"The aim is to create systems that are ecologically-sound and economically viable, which provide for their own needs, do not exploit or pollute, and are therefore sustainable in the long term...Permaculture uses the inherent qualities of plants and animals combined with the natural characteristics of landscapes and structures to produce a life-supporting system for city and country, using the smallest practical area."*
- **Bill Mollison** (Australia)
www.tagari.com

*"Permaculture offers an understanding of how biological processes are integrated, and it deals primarily with tangibles: plants, soils, water, animal systems, wildlife, bush regeneration, biotechnology, agriculture, forestry, architecture, and society in the areas of economics, land access, bioregions and incomes tied to right livelihood."*
- **Rosemary Morrow** (Australia) www.bluemountainspermacultureinstitute.com.au

*"Permaculture is an ecological design system for sustainability in all aspects of human endeavor. It teaches us how to design natural homes and abundant food production systems, regenerate degraded landscapes and ecosystems, develop ethical economies and communities, and much more. As an ecological design system, permaculture focuses on the interconnections between things more than individual parts."*
- **Scott Pittman** (USA) www.permaculture.org

*"Permaculture is about the beautiful simplicity of taking away what cannot be... decision making and problem solving protocols based on the patterns of nature."*
- **Larry Santoyo** (USA) www.permacultureacademy.com

*"Permaculture is a set of design strategies for making decisions and a set of tools for arriving at sustainable solutions."*
- **Toby Hemenway** (USA) www.tobyhemeneway.com

 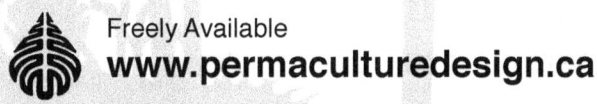

Freely Available
**www.permaculturedesign.ca**

**PERMACULTURE WORKSHEET 004**

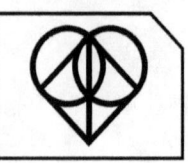

# FOUNDATIONAL CONCEPTS
## DEFINING PERMACULTURE

"*Reclaiming our place in nature as earth stewards, our sense of place, of belonging to the earth, Permaculture fosters respect for life and it's complexity, awareness of the consequences of our actions, and accepting responsibility for how we meet our needs. Permaculture draws from the wisdoms of traditional and indigenous cultures and weaves this with our contemporary knowledge of ecology, earth science and technology to create abundance, regenerate the land and build resilient communities.*

*Human creativity, passion and innovation shapes the diverse ways people apply permaculture and adapt it to local resources, climate and cultural context. Every system is unique. Permaculture empowers us in a practical way to explore and realize our potential as positive agents of change, individually and collectively.*

*Living with the challenges of the Anthropocene, permaculture provides a way forward to make our human impact meaningful, to restore the balance by being conscious consumers, to live within the earth's biocapacity and respect our interdependence with all life. Permaculture is dancing with nature, and nature leads the dance.*"
- **Robin Francis** www.permaculture.com.au

"*Permaculture is the conscious design and maintenance of agriculturally productive ecosystems which have the diversity, stability, and resilience of natural ecosystems. It is the harmonious integration of landscape and people providing their food, energy, shelter and other material and non-material needs in a sustainable way. Without permanent agriculture there is no possibility of a stable social order.*"
- **Bill Mollison** www.tagari.com

"*Permaculture is a philosophy of working with, rather than against nature; of protracted and thoughtful observation rather than protracted and thoughtless labor; and of looking at plants and animals in all their functions, rather than treating any area as a single product system.*"
- **Bill Mollison** www.tagari.com

"*Permaculture is not just about the elements in a system but the relationship between the elements - this is synergistic design.*"
- **Michael Becker** (USA) www.vimeo.com/permaculturedesigns/inspiringeducation

 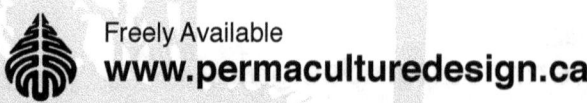

Freely Available
www.permaculturedesign.ca

**PERMACULTURE WORKSHEET 005**

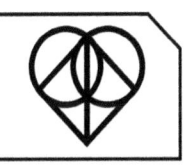

# FOUNDATIONAL CONCEPTS
## DEFINING PERMACULTURE

Basic
"*Permaculture is about creating and maintaining relationships. Developing healthy communities, permaculture people live by sharing resources and supporting each other. It begins with all the plants and animals, buildings and resources that can be found in and around your home. Permaculture is a continuing process exploring the ways in which you can fulfill the needs of the things around you while having your own needs met.*"

Intermediate
"*Permaculture is a process of growing awareness. Linking people with plants and animals, permaculture promotes conscious living, sustainable development and resource conservation. It is a response to the industrial urbanization of the Earth and resulting toxification of the biosphere. The permaculture path opens dialogues about finding creative solutions for problems in the present.*"

Advanced
"*Permaculture consciousness enhances our ability to work with maps and connect to the territory. It looks towards saving energy, conserving resources and forming long-term interdependent relationships with whole communities of living things. Permaculture develops applied understandings of the subtle implications and felt impacts of our actions on the world around us. This whole system design post-paradigm can help us to streamline the way we plan the course of human development.*"
- Delvin Solkinson (Canada) www.visionarypermaculture.com

"*Permaculture is a solution based way of life that offers opportunity to live in right relationship with the earth, its people and future generations to come. By taking a whole systems approach to design, Permaculture looks to the root of the worlds problems and seeks answers that are thoughtful, inclusive and long term with a goal of building a regenerative, healthy and thriving natural and social ecology.*"
- Kym Chi (Canada) www.gigglingchitree.com

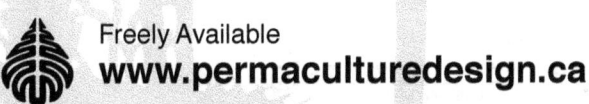

Freely Available
www.permaculturedesign.ca

PERMACULTURE WORKSHEET 006

# FOUNDATIONAL CONCEPTS
## ETHOS

Permaculture is the spirit of the age. Appropriate actions at this time include a duty to of care to look after the world and its people and build healthy foundations for the future.

The Prime Directive of Permaculture from Bill Mollison : "The only ethical decision is to take responsibility for our own existence and that of our children"

### EARTH CARE
This is the covenant we have with our world in exchange for the gift of our life. Humanity has a responsibility to love and protect the Earth. Earth Care means looking out for the holistic health of all livings things on our planet. Our mission is to repair, conserve and regenerate the Earth.

### PEOPLE CARE
Our covenant with each other is to love and protect all people. People Care means looking out for the health and welfare of our human family. Providing healthy homes, food and medicine is a part of this. Our mission is to to seek peace and guard human rights everywhere.

### FUTURE CARE
Originally Bill Mollison characterized this as two different but related ethics "Set Limits to Population and Consumption" and "Generate Surplus and Reinvest in People Care and Earth Care". At the turn of the millennium it was described as 'Fair Share', the essence of previous articulations. The African School of Permaculture brilliantly describes this as Future Care. All living things have the same inherent value and right to live a healthy life, including the generations to come. Generate an abundance and share the Earth's resources generously and equally with all things. Our mission is to invest all capital intelligence and goodwill and labour to Earth Care and People Care.

*"Passionate and Caring People are the Heart of Permaculture. People working together and sharing their journey, growing together in Community, growing food, babies, ideas, actions, groups and social enterprises, supporting healthy people and a healthy planet."*
- **Robin Clayfield** www.dynamicgroups.com.au

Freely Available
www.permaculturedesign.ca

# FOUNDATIONAL CONCEPTS
## ETHOS

**TRANSITION**
Our world is in transition and cannot become sustainable in one giant leap. In times of transition it is ok to use unsustainable means when creating a sustainable system. For example, if there is a machine available to do earth working to shape your new permaculture site, it might make more sense than spending hundreds of human hours hand digging it. What better use for the last stocks of oil than to build systems that are not dependent upon oil to work. Stop any judgement of yourself or others for being raised in an unsustainable society. Model good behaviours to teach, never blame or shame others. It helps people to move slowly with great intention, one step at a time. Learn from mistakes and commend yourself and others for the good that is done. At each new step of permaculture design, people are living in more alignment with their values.

This ethos is expressed more fully in the
**Permaculture Design : Core Concepts Cards**
available freely at www.dewpermaculture.com/tools

*"Nature and, in effect, Life and well-being, health and restoration, is the heart of permaculture practiced through conscious analysis and design*

*Permaculture must inform your work though its principles and ethics which are most adaptable to everyone else's work*

*The future of permaculture depends on teachers and its uptake. Permaculture as a curriculum has been a major success in education on a global scale. There are few curricula that can claim such broad adoption of the essential principles and features of it as an educational proposal, as permaculture does. So whether it is taken up formally, or not, it will continue to spread and sometimes acknowledged, and sometimes, not. It infiltrates all parts of life. I believe it will continue to spread and its speed of spread depends on how much people realize how few resources are left."*
- **Rosemary Morrow** www.bluemountainspermacultureinstitute.com.au

Freely Available
**www.permaculturedesign.ca**

**PERMACULTURE WORKSHEET 008**

# FOUNDATIONAL CONCEPTS
## KEY CHARACTERISTICS

- Designs involve right relationships and beneficial connections
- Develops goals, strategies and methods, not cookie cutter approaches
- Thinks at a strategic level about all the possibilities before arriving at a solution
- Can be applied to small scale land use patterns
- Favours multi functionality
- Intensive rather than extensive land use
- Promotes diversity in species, cultivars, yields, microclimates, habitats and functions
- Involves the integration of agriculture, animal husbandry, forestry, foraging, and landform engineering
- Is adaptable to edges and marginal lands
- Makes use of the naturally inherent characteristics of animal, plant and land relationships
- Uses wild and domestic species
- Values appropriate technology
- Focuses on long term sustainability
- Helps make people self-reliant
- Roles and leadership are interchangeable and revokable
- Arrives at solutions, does not impose them
- Behaves like a natural ecosystem
- Enables surrounding ecosystems to still function
- Encourages succession
- Is regenerative
- Encourages friendships and meaningful connections using social design

"We all share the same roots of permaculture from Bill Mollison and David Holmgren, that now run deep and wide and are plentifully myceliated across our precious planet. But those roots have now grown into huge trees and food forests, complete with synergistic relationships expounding the ethics and principles our community holds dear. Our unique foundations in each corner or the globe are built person by person, inspired by educators and practitioners, aided significantly by our expanding online presence. We are practicing the ethic to distribute our surpluses, often in the form of knowledge and hands-on experiences. The permaculture design certification (PDC) is still the best way to get started. It is a mind, soul, and heart opening experience, that gives the participant three unforgettable experiences: the course content, the community of teachers and students you work with, and a deep connection to the place where you have these epiphanies. One student called it "Birth-Right Knowledge" and I agree. It also opens a wide door to connect with the international permaculture community. But talking the talk is nothing if you don't walk the walk."
- Jenny Pell www.permacultureintl.com

Freely Available
www.permaculturedesign.ca

**PERMACULTURE WORKSHEET 009**

# FOUNDATIONAL CONCEPTS
## PERMACULTURE DESIGN PRINCIPLES

Nature has an operating system. This brilliant and regenerative system that cycles energy and produces no waste is based on the poly functionality of a set of design principles.

"*Permaculture principles are protocols for decision making and problem solving.*"
- **Larry Santoyo** www.permacultureacademy.com

"*Permaculture Principles are indicators of sustainability.*"
- **Toby Hemenway** www.tobyhemeneway.com

"*Apply the design principles as closely as you can you'll end up with wonderful production of good systems.*"
- **Rosemary Morrow** www.bluemountainspermacultureinstitute.com.au

The Original **12 Principles from David Holmgren** www.permacultureprinciples.com
- Observe and Interact
- Catch and Store Energy
- Obtain a yield
- Apply Self Regulation and Accept Feedback
- Use and Value Renewable Resources and Services
- Produce No Waste
- Design From Patterns to Details
- Integrate Rather Than Segregate
- Use Small and Slow Solutions
- Use and Value Diversity
- Use Edges and Value the Marginal
- Creatively Use and Respond to Change

Freely Available
**www.permaculturedesign.ca**

**PERMACULTURE WORKSHEET 010**

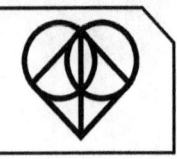

# FOUNDATIONAL CONCEPTS
## PERMACULTURE DESIGN PRINCIPLES

The original principles from Introduction to Permaculture by **Bill Mollison & Reny Mia Slay** www.tagari.com
- Relative location
- Each element performs many functions
- Each important function is supported by many elements
- Efficient energy planning: zone, sector and slope
- Use biological resources
- Cycle energy, nutrients, resources
- Small-scale intensive systems; including plant stacking and time stacking
- Accelerate succession and evolution
- Edge effect
- Everything works both ways

The one's shared from **Bill Mollison** in the Designer Manual are
- Work with nature rather than against
- The problem is the solution
- Make the least change for the greatest possible effect
- The yield of a system is theoretically unlimited, or only limited by the imagination and information of the designer
- Everything gardens by modifying its environment

Many more permaulture principles can be found in the companion card deck for this book : **Permaculture Design : Core Concepts Cards** available freely at www.dewpermaculture.com/tools

**Source Curriculum :** Bill Mollison, David Holmgren, Rosemary Morrow, Toby Hemenway, Robin Clayfield, Larry Santoyo, Michael Becker, Looby Macnamara, Scott Pittman, Geoff Lawton, Robyn Francis, Mark Lakeman, Patricia Michael, Starhawk, Bullock Brothers, Tom Ward, Jude Hobbs
**Envoy :** Delvin Solkinson www.visionarypermaculture.com
**Foundational Work :** Kym Chi www.gigglingchitree.com
**Gaiacraft Workbook Editing Team :** Delvin Solkinson, Kym Chi, Annaliese Hordern, Tamara Griffiths, Jacob Aman, Tes Tesla, Niki Hammond
**Design :** Sijay James www.onbeyondmetamedia.com

Freely Available
www.permaculturedesign.ca

**PERMACULTURE WORKSHEET 011**

# DESIGN METHODS
## ZONES

There are many permaculture methods to direct and organize your approach to the process of designing. These methods bring depth and breadth of research, consideration, logic, functionality and creativity to your designs during their inception, application and assessment. Let the principles and the design methods be a driver for your permaculture processes to help make the most effective, efficient and ethical systems.

**ZONE ANALYSIS**

Zones are areas where elements are placed according to distance from the centre of energy, frequency of use, amount of care and upkeep needed, and scale of production. When we do a zone analysis we consider each element in relation to function, structure, nutrient, energy, water and access needs.

**SELF AND BODY**
The foundation of your ability to interact with the outer zones

USE: all the time
AREA: your body
COMPONENTS: physical, emotional, spiritual, mental sensations
LIFE SYSTEMS: digestive bacterias and friendly flora, neurochemicals, hormones, enzymes and blood cells
TECHNIQUES: microclimates for food storage, integrative nutrition, exercise, conscious relationships, personal healing, massage, professional fulfillment and love
WATER: drink between 2 and 3 litres of clean, alkaline water per day
PROTECTION : from bacteria, disease, physical and mental illness
FUNCTIONS: physically strong and resilient, emotionally centred, mentally clear
GOALS : maintain overall health and self-awareness

Freely Available
www.permaculturedesign.ca

PERMACULTURE WORKSHEET 012

# DESIGN METHODS
## ZONES

**HOME**
Designed to support the Self and Body

USE: almost every day and night
AREA: living space
URBAN AREA: apartment, condo or house
COMPONENTS: kitchen, sleeping area, bathroom, communication centre
PLANTS: herbs, indoor plants for purifying air, aquaponics, worm farm, recycling station, compost pre-station
TECHNIQUES: relative location, indoor gardening, sustainable technology, insulation, greywater, low energy appliances, passive heating, recycling
WATER: locate 'wet rooms' kitchen, laundry, bathroom to be able to get greywater to garden, water catchment and storage, grey water treatment, utilize waterless toilets
ANIMALS: pets to provide companionship, protection and eat scraps
PROTECTION : from elements and climatic factors, security from invaders
FUNCTIONS: a climate regulated, safe place to live, love, eat, sleep and work
GOALS: conserve energy, save heat, produce some food, store food, process food, provide all energy needed from within the system, non-polluting or creating waste, non-consuming, non-toxic, using renewable energies, passive solar, lit by natural daylight all day, form (design) and function match, local materials if possible, meet its own needs for energy and water and food

Freely Available
www.permaculturedesign.ca

PERMACULTURE WORKSHEET 013

# DESIGN METHODS
## ZONES

**GARDEN**
Intensively cultivated and cared for

USE: daily
AREA: space immediately surrounding the home
URBAN AREA: yard
COMPONENTS: small greenhouse, trellis, patio, bird feeder, workshop, storage, bathroom, cold frames, worm compost bin, small compost station, propagation area, stone wall, shade house, vegetable garden, fencing, shed, clipping beds, plucking beds, board and narrow beds, tiny pond, windbreak, keyhole, mandala and dome beds
PLANTS: herbs, salad greens, flowers, soft fruit, dwarf trees, low shrubs, tender annual veggies
TECHNIQUES: intensive planting, sheet mulching, dense planting, espaliering, abundant and diverse plantings, functional pathways
WATER: rain barrel, small ponds, grey water, back up drinking water storage, rain water catchment, grey & black water treatment, compost toilet, aquaculture, small gardens
WATERING: intensive irrigation
ANIMALS: wild birds, rabbits, guinea pigs, soil organisms, beneficial insects, small animals help with weeding and maintenance
FOOD SHED: home garden
ENERGY SHED: energy captured and stored on your property, recycle compost and waste from the house
PROTECTION : from elements, climatic factors and animals
FUNCTIONS: modify house, create and utilize microclimates, daily food and flowers, social space, meet needs of garden for nutrient
GOALS: reduce energy and water needs, harness natural resources, create a harmonious place to love, live, work and play, meet 80% of household foods, limit maintenance required, keep monitoring system

Freely Available
www.permaculturedesign.ca

PERMACULTURE WORKSHEET 014

# DESIGN METHODS
## ZONES

**FOOD FOREST**
Semi-intensive cultivation and care

USE: visited almost everyday
AREA: area just beyond the garden
URBAN AREA: walking distance 'pedosphere'
COMPONENTS: larger greenhouse, barn, tool shed, shop, wood storage, smoke house, large compost, small orchard, chicken coop, beehives, fire break
PLANTS: staple and canning food, fruits and nut trees
TECHNIQUES: heavy mulching, cover crops, seasonal pruning, drying and smoking food, stacking of plants, multi-purpose walk throughs, free ranging poultry, high diversity of plants, nutrient from green manures and living mulches, polycultural orchard guilds, floral pasture, windbreaks to prevent drying out from winds and to protect yields
WATER: well, pond, irrigation, swales, back up systems, ripping, terracing, ditches, net and pan, fire defence, wind deflection, safeguarding animals and pest reduction, small earthworks, water bodies for reflecting light
WATERING: intensive irrigation
ANIMALS: rabbits, fish, bats, poultry, animals help to prune, fertilize, scratch, control pests and provide local small protein option
FOOD SHED: neighbours, CSA, community garden
ENERGY SHED: energy captured and stored in your community
PROTECTION: wind, hail and snow
FUNCTIONS: home food production, local food resiliency, market crops, plant propagation, wildlife habitat
GOALS: intensive production, cycling energy

Freely Available
www.permaculturedesign.ca

PERMACULTURE WORKSHEET 015

# DESIGN METHODS
## ZONES

**FARM**
Semi-frequent seasonal cultivation and care

USE: visited every couple of days, very little in off-season
AREA: broad scale land base
URBAN AREA: biking distance 'cyclosphere'
COMPONENTS: feed storage, field shelters, main perennial crops, large orchard, grazing fields, windbreaks, firebreaks
PLANTS: cash crops, large fruit and nut trees, animal forage, shelterbelts, hedgerows
TECHNIQUES: cover crops, little pruning, movable fences, spot mulching, diverse forage, pasture cropping, alley cropping
WATER: large ponds, swales, diversion channels, contour ripping, treelines, dams with spillways, key point dam diversions
WATERING: light irrigation
ANIMALS: cows, horses, pigs, sheep, goats, large animals, animals eat surplus and fertilize the ground
FOOD SHED: farm gate, farmers market
ENERGY SHED: energy captured and stored in your region
PROTECTION : from climate, predators, fire, invasive species, toxins
FUNCTIONS: market crops, firewood, lumber
GOALS: high yields, energy efficiency, regeneration, storage, back up systems, good planning, products for market and distribution, rehydrate the land, earn an income

Freely Available
www.permaculturedesign.ca

# DESIGN METHODS
## ZONES

**WOODLAND**
Minimal care

USE: visited weekly
AREA: area beyond the farm zone
URBAN AREA: reachable by bus or short drive
COMPONENTS: open pasture, cultivated woodland, dams, wind mills
PLANTS: firewood, timber, native plants, non-timber forest products, mushrooms, medicine plants, food, forage
TECHNIQUES: pasturing, controlled burns, hand transplanting, selective forestry, coppice managed woodland, long term tree planting, understory plantings, green mulching, plant around the fences, start with pioneering nitrogen fixing trees which are eventually cut and mulched, plant high value short use timbers next to the nitrogen fixers for firewood, tools. poles, fences, short, plant high value longer term timbers in woodland for construction beams and feature long thick boards, start edges with berries and short trees
WATER: ponds, lake, river, wetlands, reforestation, watershed management is a must for rural areas
ANIMALS: grazing and protecting space, fixed and mobile species, large animals like cattle, deer, pigs, sheep, turkeys, goats, and wild animals
FOOD SHED: independent grocer with regional focus
ENERGY SHED: energy imported from neighbouring regions
PROTECTION : logging, trespassing, poaching, fire, wild animals
FUNCTIONS: hunting, gathering, grazing, wildcrafting, selective logging, forestry, long term development
GOALS : make good use of the land requiring minimal maintenance, animals supply nutrients to forest, diverse yields and functions, stores carbon, filters light, mycelium based, planting for the future, multiple benefits

Freely Available
www.permaculturedesign.ca

PERMACULTURE WORKSHEET 017

# DESIGN METHODS
## ZONES

**WILD FOREST**
Unmanaged nature

USE: weekly or monthly
AREA: natural space beyond all developments, around rivers, and on slopes over 18%
URBAN AREA: reachable only by plane or long-distance transport
COMPONENTS: wildlife corridors
PLANTS: native plants, indigenous forest, ground covers, prickly plants
TECHNIQUES: unmanaged, erosion control, natural barrier, plant back original vegetation, start in the middle and work out, vegetation to prevent erosion, branch scatter and hand forecast tree seeds or use pellet bombs
WATER: lake, creek, rehydrate the landscape and replenish the aquifer
ANIMALS: native animal reserve habitat, extend wildlife corridors
FOOD SHED: chain supermarket featuring health food isle
ENERGY SHED: energy imported from another country
PROTECTION : logging, trespassing, poaching, fire, wild animals, human with domestic cat and dog impact
FUNCTIONS: inspiration, nature preserve, observational learning
GOALS: preserve true nature without interfering, restore native habitat, stabilize soil and water, maintain wildlife corridors, replant the ecosystem, recharge rivers and aquifers, minimum disturbance, ideally 30-45% of broad scale land is under perennial systems and 70% is designated as native forest. Rosemary Morrow says to find the more desireable spot on the landscape and protect it instead of developing it

Freely Available
www.permaculturedesign.ca

# DESIGN METHODS
## SECTORS

Sector mapping identifies and tracks the movement of energies and influences from outside that come onto, or through, the design site. Sectors may be shown visually on a map using colors and arrows marking the source and direction of flow. Sectors include visible energies like sun, water and wind as well as invisible influences like politics, neighbours, building codes, social trends, crime, easements, zoning bylaws and building codes. Sector patterns may change hourly, daily, weekly, monthly and seasonally. Micro-sectors note specific detailed information about sectors. Designing for sectors gives you the option to block, channel, or capture and store the energies and influences you identify.

**SUN** : The sun rise and set changes in different seasons. Identify hours of sun, shade and dappled light on your land. Walk around on a sunny day every hour from dawn till dusk to get a super accurate sun micro-sector map.

**WIND** : Note seasonal patterns of prevailing cool and warm winds. Where are the wind channels or wind breaks. Walk around on a windy day to chart wind micro-sector.

**WATER** : Identify taps and water access points. Track the flow of running water and note drainage in seasonal brooks, streams, rivers, dams, and creeks. Also locate standing water like ponds, lakes, marshes, wells, rain barrels, swales, and damp soil areas. Look for patterns of erosion on the property and consider how you can reroute or block. Walk around after its been raining for a day or two and look for damp areas or standing water to get detailed micro-sector analysis. Cherish and protect springs.

**FROST** : Cool air moves downhill and stays in low lying areas condensing as frost on cold mornings. Note frost pockets by doing a micro-sector map on a frosty morning.

**PEOPLE AND ANIMAL MOVEMENT** : Note movement of animals and people through the property. This may indicate existing pathways, roads or driveways, or show where these should be added.

Freely Available
www.permaculturedesign.ca

**PERMACULTURE WORKSHEET 019**

# DESIGN METHODS
## SECTORS

**NOISE** : Where is noise coming from? Listen for pleasant and unpleasant noises. Micro-sectors for noise may include identifying daily or even hourly noise patterns that can be heart on your site.

**SMELLS** : Pay attention to pleasant and unpleasant scents and note where they might be coming from. Document the times of day or times of year when you notice these smells. Check wind sector.

**FIRE** : Fire usually comes up a hill or from the direction of your hot summer winds. Dry areas like grasslands may be pathways for fires to travel. Sometimes fires behaves unusually in hills and gullies. Look into the history bushfires or forest fires in your area to learn more about fire sectors.

**ENERGY** : Locate water, gas and electric lines and shutoffs.

**MICROCLIMATES** : Explore the site looking for small differences in temperature, sun, shade, dampness, slope, exposure or soil type.

**URBAN** : Look at boundaries where people or animals may come onto the site or places that crime or vandalism might be an issue.

**DISASTER** : Are you in danger of earthquakes, tsunamis, hurricanes / typhoons, lightning, extreme weather, industrial pollution,
nuclear fallout or any other nature or man made disaster? Plan for 100 year disaster or climactic events.

**VIEW** : From different places on site, where are the ugly or beautiful views?

Gaiacraft shares a plethora of design methods in the
Gaiacraft Permaculture Design : Core Concepts Cards
available freely at www.gaiacraft.com

Freely Available
www.permaculturedesign.ca

**PERMACULTURE WORKSHEET 020**

# DESIGN METHODS
## MAPPING PROJECT

Permaculture Mapping deepens our conscious connection with our world. Observing a design site for at least a full year of seasonal changes, we can learn so much about what is already going on, and what might be appropriate elements to move around, add or take away.

Creating a **MAP FOLIO** can help you stay organized and contain all your notes, observations, ideas and design visions. Documenting the process of applying any designs is beneficial. This folio may include :

**BASE MAP** includes all the elements on your site such as
- structures
- pathways
- contours
- water
- trees
- plants
- gardens
- resources

Using Google Earth or mapping software from the mapping department of your local government website can help you get a traceable photograph from space showing your property. If you go into the local regional district offices directly, there is usually a mapping department who will provide you free maps of your watershed, property boundaries and many other features.

**PLANT AND ANIMAL LIST** includes any animals that live on or pass through your design site throughout the year. Creating food and habitats for beneficial animals can encourage them to be around even more.

Try to get the exact species of plants and animals using ID books. If possible see if you can photograph special plants and animals to help illustrated your map folio. Any plants that you can't identify, you could try taking a leaf and flower into a large nursery or botanical gardens, for correct identification.

Freely Available
www.permaculturedesign.ca

**PERMACULTURE WORKSHEET 021**

# DESIGN METHODS
## MAPPING PROJECT

*"As far as plant ID goes, I also think that once you have a positive ID, it is very helpful, after sending a gratitude to the plant, to snap off a small branch. Is the stem hollow or solid? Does it give off a scent? Ooze or sap? Hold a leaf in your mouth - is it faintly fuzzy? What else is it giving off? Bite down and lick your teeth, it is super difficult to poison yourself with such a tiny amount, but it will stimulate many different parts of your brain to 'know' and remember that particular plant. Pick several different grape leaves and line them up, or different strawberry leaves, you will slowly see the very subtle differences. This will just help your book learning."*
- Robin Wheeler www.onestraw.ca

**ZONE MAP** allows you to apply the zone analysis and look at elements relative to their use, maintenance, scale and distance from the places you spend the most time.

**MICRO-SECTOR MAP** brings you awareness of the energies and influences passing onto or through the design site. Once you identify the micro-sectors you may want to block the energy from entering, allow it to come through easier, channel it through the site in a specific way, or even capture and store the energy for future use. Consider doing a sector analysis each season. Later you might even do one in every month.

*"The root question is : How do we get reconnected with the Earth?*
*Become ecologically literate in your place and your home.*
*Learn how to grow food.*
*Where is your food coming from?*
*Where is your water coming from and what are your water harvesting capabilities?*
*Where is your waste stream going?*
*Learn the systems that you live in.*
*How can you create as resilient a system as possible with what you have within your community?*
*What makes sense for you to do yourself?*
*What makes sense for you to engage in your greater community?.*
*Getting active with local governments is important.*
*Look at what other communities you can reach out to and collaborate with.*
*What is the vision that you are holding?"*
- Penny Livingston-Stark www.regenerativedesign.org

Freely Available
www.permaculturedesign.ca

**PERMACULTURE WORKSHEET 022**

# DESIGN METHODS
## MAPPING PROJECT

**SUN** : Walk through the site every hour from dawn till dusk on a sunny day noting sun, shade and dapple light.

**WIND** : Go out on a windy day and note the wind channels on the land or places where there is no wind. You can also note general directions the seasonal winds come from. Research where the dominant winds come from.

**WATER** : Walk around in the rain after a heavy rainfall. Note any pooling or running water as well as seasonally wet soil. Chart frost sectors on a frosty morning.

**NOISE** : Explore your design site notice where noise comes from and when.

**SMELLS**: Explore your design site, notice where scents come from and when they can be smelt.

**MOVEMENT** : Sit quietly and observe the movement of people and animals across the land.

**VIEWS** : Look for any great views or ugly ones.

**MICROCLIMATE** : Note niche areas of differing temperature, moisture, soil, slope, exposure or unique vegetation. Identify microclimates evident around structures.

What other micro-sectors can you observe and charge on your map. Look at physical factors as well as non-physical influences.

**Source Curriculum:** Bill Mollison, David Holmgren, Rosemary Morrow, Toby Hemenway, Robin Clayfield, Larry Santoyo, Michael Becker, Looby Macnamara, Scott Pittman, Geoff Lawton, Robyn Francis, Mark Lakeman, Patricia Michael, Starhawk, Bullock Brothers, Tom Ward, Jude Hobbs

**Envoy:** Delvin Solkinson www.visionarypermaculture.com

**Foundational Work :** Kym Chi www.gigglingchitree.com

**Gaiacraft Workbook Editing Team :** Delvin Solkinson, Kym Chi, Annaliese Hordern, Tamara Griffiths, Jacob Aman, Tes Tesla, Niki Hammond

**Design :** Sijay James www.onbeyondmetamedia.com

Freely Available
www.permaculturedesign.ca

**PERMACULTURE WORKSHEET 023**

# PATTERN LITERACY
## WORLD CODE

The natural world of forms and processes, as well as the human world of behaviours, is made of patterns. Patterns can teach us how to design.

**PATTERN RECOGNITION** : Cultivating our senses to be able to identify patterns and recognize their functions.

**PATTERN LITERACY** : Seeing the world as made of patterns which are functional and dysfunctional, then applying that understanding to the way you make decisions and design. Pattern understanding can help us remember vast amounts of knowledge. Learn to recognize patterns of casualty and anchor in functional patterns while replacing dysfunctional ones.

**STACKING PATTERNS** : Patterns occur like fractals; on all scales, in time and in space.

**READING THE LANDSCAPE** : Relearning the pattern language of nature to see how all plants and animals are indicators of climate and rich sources of information about the bioregion that guide us in conscious design.

*"The foundation of Permaculture is keen observation. Bill Mollison and David Holmgren read the land with such intensity that they came up with a design system that mimics nature. They watched, and documented the inter-relationships of all elements and designed whole functioning systems; catching water to enhance life, utilizing biomass to build soil, considering the right plant in the right place and continuing this pattern of application within a sites' component framework*

*The goal is to create conditions that yield to desired outcomes such as creating year round beauty, productivity and potential income. Follow the steps toward passion based learning in any realm that interests you. Ask critical thinking questions weighing the options and assessing opportunities to minimize work and maximize effect. Learn a diversity of design skills that generate confidence. Be brave, learn from your mistakes.*

*As William McDonough says : 'Designers forecast the future'. Consider the concept of Right Livelihood. Conscious planning yields abundance in all aspects of life. Go forth and plork (play/work)."*
- **Jude Hobbs** www.cascadiapermaculture.com

Freely Available
**www.permaculturedesign.ca**

**PERMACULTURE WORKSHEET 024**

# PATTERN LITERACY
## FUNCTIONS

### SPIRAL
Allows for growth and movement. Uniformly fills space and maximizes material holding potential. Increases exchange, transport and helps with anchoring. Enables things to move against gravity. Concentrates or disperses, speeds up or slows down flow depending on which direction the spiral is moving.

### BRANCHING
Enables the collection and distribution of materials and resources. An efficient way to reach many points in an area while traveling the shortest distance.

### SCATTER
Helps energy release and the ability to spread material quickly. The place where the scattered seeds or materials land is the scatter pattern.

### WAVE
Allows for movement, circulation and transportation. The pattern of a heartbeat.

### CIRCLES WITHIN CIRCLES
Stabilizes and protects. Allows objects or social structures to be stacked on inside another.

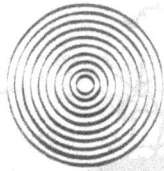

### WEB
A resilient system made of nodes and links. If one node or link is broken it does not destroy the pattern. It conserves space, resources, time and energy. Is good for collection, filtering and small surface exchange.

Freely Available
www.permaculturedesign.ca

# PATTERN LITERACY
## FUNCTIONS

### SPHERE
Balance inner and outer forces. Offers the most volume for the least amount of surface area. Minimizes heat loss and is easy to roll.

### STAR
Radiates and pulses energy. Expands and spreads.

### STREAMLINE
Allows for effective flow of fluids and gases past fixed bodies.

### SCALE
Creates strength while remaining flexible.

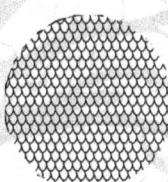

### LOBE
Increases energy transfer across surfaces. Provides a longer edge surface for growth.

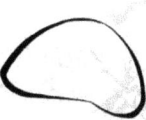

### OVERBECK JET
Enables the natural streaming of gases and fluids past objects or forms. Generates vortices and spirals.

Freely Available
www.permaculturedesign.ca

PERMACULTURE WORKSHEET 026

# PATTERN LITERACY
## WORLD CODE

**ORDERS** : Every pattern has orders from large to small. Each time you move between orders, you half the size and material being delivered. Orders indicate changes in size or scale and are a measure of size, volume or concentration contained within the same form or pattern. Orders are related to gathering and dispersing of contents (eg. nutrients, waste, energy flows). Orders are numbered from 1 - 7 but may be as few as 5. As the order decreases the flow slows down. Order 1 is substantial, sluggish and has inertia, it's larger and slower. Order 6 or 7 is fast and turbulent :  it's smaller and faster.

**NETWORK PATTERNS** : Every element in every order is a node in a network pattern. All feeding relationships, social relationships and nutrient cycles are networks. They consist of two elements: links and nodes. Networks are very resilient if they have many nodes. Networks are very hard to destroy because they are non-hierarchical and you can remove many links and nodes and still not destroy the whole structure. For example Bees are links in a network where trees and flowering plants are the nodes. Bees pollinate about 1/3 of the worlds food supply. The greater the number of bees the stronger the network. In our ecosystem nitrogen fixing trees are key nodes and mycelium are key links.

"Although permaculture draws on the wisdom of nature and traditional cultures of place, its innovative, experimental, DIY design approach to the novel and challenging contexts of the modern world makes it much more than any restoration of tradition. From damaged and degraded landscapes to novel ecosystems, from discarded rubbish to creative reuse and dysfunctional and dependent consumerism to empowered personal and community productivity permaculture combines the best from traditions and our globally shared culture of recent decades of innovation.

If the long predicted and progressively unfolding Limits to Growth crises (energy, climate and economy) shift the world towards the Energy Descent future, then interest in permaculture will accelerate, whether or the "permaculture" brand survives. In the same way that many strategies and techniques already popularised through permaculture from mulching and worm farms to bushfire resilient design or local currencies, the radical shift to a relocalised economy with larger numbers of people involved in food production and self reliance is an inevitable part of the Energy Descent future. Permaculture shows how we can survive and thrive in a future than many people fear and refuse to accept."
- **David Holmgren** www.holmgren.com.au

Freely Available
www.permaculturedesign.ca

**PERMACULTURE WORKSHEET 027**

# PATTERN LITERACY
## GUILDS

A guild is a collection of living and non-living things that work together symbiotically, where the products and outputs of one, fulfill the needs of another.

Here are some functions that plants can play in a garden guild :

**FOOD PRODUCER** : Creates edible food for people, plants, insects or animals. Ensures that the guild is valuable to maintain and protect.

**MEDICINE PRODUCER** : Provide medicine for people, animals, insects and plants. Ensures the guild is healthy.

**MULCH** : Covers the soil, provides nutrients and organic matter, moderates temperature and climactic effects, suppresses weeds, retains water, builds soil and prevents erosion.

**LIVING MULCH** : Frances Michaels coined this term to describe perennial herbaceous plants cover the soil typically in an orchard system. They provide nitrogen to soil and soil organisms, improve soil by breaking it up with their roots, allowing greater water infiltration and retention, reduce evaporation while protecting soil from erosion. An inoculant introducing symbiotic bacteria to assist successful growth is often required. Living mulches keep soil cooler in the summer and warmer in the winter, moderating climatic effects and reduce competition from weed species. These plants often provide bee forage and attract beneficial pests. When cut or sythed, living mulches return nutrients to the soil.

**GREEN MANURE** : Frances Michaels also talks about a green herb layer of legumes and grasses are used to provide nitrogen and organic matter to the soil and prepare soil for planting crops. Typically the layer is slashed or dug into the soil while green, before seed develops and is left to return these nutrients to the soil. Used to out compete weeds.

**ATTRACTORS** : Bring in pollinators or other creatures that are beneficial to the guild or surrounding gardens. These insects perform tasks such as pollination, seed distribution and planting as well as predating on pests.

**REPEL PESTS** : Help to discourage or repel pests or predators that threaten the healthy functioning of the guild.

Freely Available
www.permaculturedesign.ca

PERMACULTURE WORKSHEET 028

# PATTERN LITERACY
## GUILDS

**NUTRIENT BIO-ACCUMULATORS** : Absorb, increase and store high levels of nutrients and minerals.

**NITROGEN FIXERS** : Participate with particular soil microorganisms to fix nitrogen into the soil. When their foliage is chopped or eaten by above-ground animals, the plants roots recess causing nitrogen to be released into the soil.

**SPIKE ROOT PLANTS** : Have roots and tubers that decompact and oxygenate the soil, allowing more air and water in.

**HABITAT CREATION** : Providing habitat for other native plants, animals or insects is a key support for the larger ecology.

**AIR PURIFICATION** : High biomass plants that breathe carbon dioxide and produce oxygen that help clean and cycle our atmosphere for humans and animals to breathe.

**WATER PURIFICATION** : Filter water and draw out toxins. These can be very helpful in cleaning rain or greywater.

**BIOREMEDIATION** : Draw up heavy metals and other toxins from the soil to help remediating areas where life is hampered by such toxicity.

**USEFUL PLANTS** : As gardeners, we have lots of reasons to care for and protect guilds containing plants that can provide material for fuel, building, tool making, providing fibre for weaving or playing any other productive functions.

**SACRIFICE SPECIES** : Give food and habitat for pests so they don't bother other plants.

**BANKER PLANTS** : Attract and provide habitat for pests in order to provide a year round food supply for beneficial predators.

Freely Available
www.permaculturedesign.ca

# PATTERN LITERACY
## GUILD DESIGN METHODS

**DESIGN BY STRUCTURE**
Organizing elements by what fits well together.

**DESIGN BY EXCLUSION**
Apply filters to reduce design options, until all that remains is the answer.

**DESIGN BY ANALOGY**
Be inspired by what is observed in native plant communities.

**DESIGN BY FUNCTION**
Combine elements that play complimentary functions.

*"Do what you love and what brings you alive, first. Find a place where your innate abilities are needed; my own personal prayer for this is, "Send me people I can help." Then apply permaculture's ethics and principles to what you are doing to shape it into something resilient and regenerative. There's plenty of work to be done; find the part of it that you are here to do, that keeps you excited. Don't limit it to "I must become a teacher, or designer." Help show that permaculture design can be applied anywhere, in any discipline. Be a model of it yourself.*

*Not to be called permaculture any more; just to be called "the way we do things." If we manage to stay here as a species, it's what we'll be doing, whatever we call it. At its core, it is not an ideology or dogma, but a way to follow the patterns that life has worked out over 4 billion years. If human life has a future here, it will create conditions conducive to more life, and that is permaculture's goal."*
- Toby Hemenway www.tobyhemenway.com

**Source Curriculum:** Bill Mollison, David Holmgren, Rosemary Morrow, Toby Hemenway, Robin Clayfield, Larry Santoyo, Michael Becker, Looby Macnamara, Scott Pittman, Geoff Lawton, Robyn Francis, Mark Lakeman, Patricia Michael, Starhawk, Bullock Brothers, Tom Ward, Jude Hobbs, Marian Farrior, Frances Michaels

**Envoy:** Delvin Solkinson www.visionarypermaculture.com

**Foundational Work :** Kym Chi www.gigglingchitree.com

**Gaiacraft Workbook Editing Team :** Delvin Solkinson, Kym Chi, Annaliese Hordern, Tamara Griffiths, Jacob Aman, Tes Tesla, Niki Hammond

**Design :** Sijay James www.onbeyondmetamedia.com

Freely Available
www.permaculturedesign.ca

# DESIGN FOR SOIL
## LIFE ALCHEMY

Soil is life. Plants are fed by the soil. To have healthy plants we need to cultivate a healthy soil. Biodynamics notes that we can feed the soil and let the soil feed the plants. This means having an awareness of the soil ecology and how to best serve its needs.

Here are some of the aspects of the soil ecology:
- Primary decomposers like bacteria, fungi, millipedes, wood bugs and worms eat composting material when it is wet. They eat the softer material and create deposits of rich food for other creatures to digest.
- Secondary decomposers like mold mites and beetles live on the primary decomposers leaving deposits of a more dynamic food.
- Tertiary decomposers like centipedes, beetles, ants, and spiders, feed on both primary and secondary decomposers yielding a third level of processed materials.
In the end, these three food deposits and the remaining hard organic matter combine to form complex molecules of humus which are broken down slowly, particularly when the soil is low in nutrient. Humus expands and contracts when it gets wet, aerating the soil while holding water and releasing water. It is from these deposits of partially digested and broken down material that most plants feed. How plants gain their nutrients provides a greater insight into the ecological process. Plants excrete acids which break down humus and release the nutrients available to plants in the right amounts. At the same time many plants secrete exudates including sugars, proteins, carbohydrates and minerals which bacteria and fungi eat. These microbial bacteria and fungi excrete antibiotics that protect plants from disease as well as acids and enzymes that help break down humus further so the plants can share in the nutrient yield. In this way a symbiotic circle is developed between plants and soil organisms. All soil micro-organisms play a diverse role in sustaining the whole ecology. For example, some bacteria secrete gums, gels and waxes that help hold the soil together, assist the absorption of water and store nutrients. Most of what is digested and transformed into living matter is carbon containing molecules. Carbon is the building block of organic life. Undigested materials include many soluble minerals which are held in the soil by humus and soil organisms. Healthy soil is alive, actively growing and recycling, breathing and digesting. This is the great recycling system of the Earth. One teaspoon of healthy soil contains a billion bacteria, a million fungi, and ten thousand amoebae. Let's celebrate again the incredible role worms play. They consume dead plant material and rocks using a combination of bacteria and grinding gizzards in their gut. Worms produces nutrient rich castings which they spread through the soil as they move around creating tunnels that aerate the ground. They will be a focus in the composting processes we do. Remember healthy soil will fulfill the wildest dreams of any plant.

Freely Available
www.permaculturedesign.ca

# DESIGN FOR SOIL
## COMPOSTING

The reason synthetic fertilizers are dangerous is that they flood the soil with an over saturation of minerals. The fertilizer that cannot be absorbed gets into the water table and can drain in concentrated forms to the nearby ecology. Unbalanced soil can attract disease in plants and animals. Also over fertilizing can create a frenzy of activity by micro-organisms, giving them a burst of energy to process many of the humus and other nutrients in the soil. Although this may give a greater production in the soil for one season, it will ultimately deplete the soil of nutrient, create a dependence on fertilizers and produce an unhealthy soil ecology.
- Dark colored compost enables the soil to warm up quicker leading to faster germination of plants, particularly in greenhouse or cold frame environments
- Heat the compost to 70 degrees celsius for a few days and all weed seeds and roots will be destroyed
- Limestone is often added to reduce acidity, help the worms digestive system and aid in the conversion of ammonia to nitrates. This assists the activities of microorganisms by breaking down clay elements and binding sandy elements. An easy way to get lime is grinding up dried eggshells.
- Adding charcoal to the bottom of the compost will absorb poisonous gasses and sweeten the heap

### SOIL CREATURES
- Bacteria and micro-organisms help break up the compost
- Aerobic bacteria breathe air and break materials into a sweet smelling soil and are connected with the decomposition process
- Anaerobic bacteria exist without oxygen and often break materials into a smelly sludge and are connected with the rotting process
- Fungi are key workers in the compost that break down harder, ligneous material and allow bacteria to gain access to it
- Protozoa are single celled organisms including amoebas, flagellates, and ciliates. These eat bacteria and fungi, releasing nitrogen and other nutrients into the soil
- Arthropods are beetles, spiders, millipedes and centipedes and other invertebrates that break down organic material allowing bacteria and fungi easier access
- Worms digest and break down organic matter including rocks, releasing a high nutrient water soluble casting which contains accessible food for many creatures and plants. With gizzards in their gut, worms produce nutrient rich castings which they spread through the soil as they move around creating tunnels that aerate the ground.
- Snails and slugs eat organic material and add slime to the soil that helps it hold together and retain moisture

Freely Available
www.permaculturedesign.ca

# DESIGN FOR SOIL
## COMPOSTING

Nature cycles energy and creates no waste. Modelled on nature, permaculture composting helps support the healthy breakdown and reuse of all organic elements.

Composting is the science of renewable systems. It shows us what materials it is sustainable to use as well as how to effectively break those materials down into rich, healthy soil, mulch, and fertilizer. Our task is composting the old culture to provide energy and resources to build the new one.

In the Cool Climates, a simple cold compost is made by alternating layers of green material (nitrogen rich organic waste like grass clippings, kitchen waste, coffee grounds, tea bags, manure, garden weeds and other fresh vegetable matter) and brown material (carbon rich organic waste like leaves, dried grasses, or hay). Match the green and brown material for production of a heavy amendment or add more brown material for a higher organic matter soil. When you add any amount of new compost material, throw in some dead leaves, grass or newspaper to help with the decomposition process. Tougher materials like wood, blackberries, egg shells or fruit pits can be put into a different pile nearby the compost to be used for hugelkultur beds later. You may wish to avoid composting meat scraps, bones or any food (cooked or uncooked) that contains dairy, wheat, oil or fats as these materials rot instead of decomposing, creating stink and attracting rodents, flies and other pests. In order to have a steady supply of brown, carbonaceous material to use in layering the compost, collect of pile up brown materials like leaves and grass clippings next to the compost. The fall is the best time to gather this supply since there are so many dead leaves. If you are using manure, or have weed seeds in the compost, you may want to allow the compost to heat to at least 70 degrees celcius.

Freely Available
www.permaculturedesign.ca

# DESIGN FOR SOIL
## COMPOST DESIGN

- Make good homes for decomposers; worms, pill bugs and millions of micro-organisms.
- Promote oxygen and airflow, allowing decomposers to breath and CO2 to leave the soil. Proper airflow also prevents the compost from breeding stinkies by creating an environment friendly to aerobic air loving micro-organisms.
- Create the ideal amount of water content. Water dissolves and carries soil nutrients to plant roots, allowing decomposers to move around. The compost should be as wet as a rung out sponge, having a thin layer of moisture coating everything and making it easier for the decomposers to do their work. If it is too dry the microbes, worms and bugs will all die. If it is too wet the compost will become compacted, anaerobic and not have proper air flow. When it has good drainage and a lid with small drip holes to let a little rain in, the compost may never need additional watering.
- Protect from the climate, too much rain, wind, sun or snow using a lid.
- Create wonderful habitat that is warm, dark and damp.
- The decomposition process generates heat. The hotter your compost is, the faster the decomposition will take place. Turning the compost will heat it up as will adding manure or meat. A lid on the compost prevents it from losing too much heat. The more you turn a compost, the quicker it will decompose but the less nutrient it will have in it since the decomposers will have used more of it in their processing. If you don't turn your compost, and its properly layered with green and brown materials, it will take longer to decompose but be richer in the end.
- Adding meat can attract rodents so meat is often added to "Bokashi" composting systems, an aerobic fermentation process that can happen in a sealed container inside your home.

*"Permaculture restores remnant woodlands, conserves forests, and places all human and animal needs with attentiveness to permanence. It repairs marginal land, values waterways, and cares for all the elements in the environment that Life needs, such as water, food and shelter. Care of people entails the Care of the Earth. Care for Earth is about putting back more than we take out. When I watch the hay coming off a field, I think about what we going to replace it with, otherwise it's still mining. The road to restoration is putting back more than we take. The restorative ethic is inherent in permaculture and is basic to all natural and designed systems. This is the way forward."*
- **Rosemary Morrow** www.bluemountainspermacultureinstitute.com.au

Freely Available
www.permaculturedesign.ca

PERMACULTURE WORKSHEET 034

# DESIGN FOR SOIL
## COMPOST CREATION

Compost can be made using three large wooden boxes or dedicated spaces on the ground. The first is where you start your compost. The second to make a second compost while the first compost is decomposing. The third to hold brown materials in storage.

A compost creates an ideal environment for worms, micro-organisms and other decomposers. Composting promotes the efficient break down of organic waste into rich fertilizing soil. Place the compost somewhere shaded, as this will slow down evaporation and allow the compost to remain damp. The boxes can have lids on hinges with 1/4 inch slats or drip holes to allow rainwater in. The sides of the boxes can have 3/4 inch spaces between the boards to allow air flow in to support the aerobic (air loving) decomposers. Line the structure with fine mesh wiring to keep rodents out. The front of the composts can be made with a removable slat system, so you can take the front off board by board to access the compost material easier than having to reach in from the top. The third brown storage box does not have slats to let in water or extra oxygen. Here you can store brown material like leaves and brown grass for later layering with green materials.

Start the compost process by laying cardboard over the base then cover this in rocks and sticks for drainage along with wood ash to sweeten the pile. Any living plants there will turn into soil and attract worms up into the system. Start with a layer of about 18 - 20 cm of mostly green plant waste. Then follow with a small layer of soil or manure. This will inoculate the pile with micro-organisms. On top of this place a layer of about 18 - 20cm of brown material such as leaves. Biodynamic plants or preparations can be added into the layers. Continue with roughly balanced amounts of green and brown to get a heavy, rich fertilizing soil amendment.

Freely Available
www.permaculturedesign.ca

**PERMACULTURE WORKSHEET  035**

# DESIGN FOR SOIL
## VERMICULTURE

A composting process using worms to assist in decomposing organic and food wastes into a biologically rich 'vermicompost' and 'worm tea'. Both of these products can be used as a wonderful soil and plant fertilizer. A vermiculture system can be located in the compost area or inside a structure. This can be built from a wood, metal, glass or fibreglass box, container or sink, and be inside or outside. Create an outdoor system by using a raised sink covered by a lid with small holes in it, and a bucket underneath. Rain drips through the small holes in the lid and percolates down through the worm farm and drips into the bucket below to collect a potent liquid fertilizer. The worm compost material can be sifted to yield rich worm-castings, used directly to fertilize soil. This worm sink or bin can be layered with newspaper and kitchen scraps such as uncooked and cooked organic vegetable matter like old salad greens, carrots and potatoes (including peels), pulp from the juicer, tea and coffee grounds, grass clippings, as well as composting super plants to assist speeding up this dynamic process. Avoid meat, citrus, dairy, onion, spicy and processed foods, fats, oils and shiny paper. Feed worms with tender greens and other nutrient rich plants. Worms often tend towards mild flavours but will eat most things. Biodynamic plants of different combinations can be added to enrich the fertilizer in many different ways. The worms can be fed up to 2.5cm/day - only add food as it is eaten. The finer the inputs the easier the worms can consume them. If the compost begins to dry out, sprinkle it with water. Put a bucket under the sink or tub to collect the drips of fertilizing worm juice. Check the bucket under the worm bin semi regularly, put it in a watering can diluting it 1:10 (1 part worm juice to 10 parts water) and apply it to your gardens - watch for the difference it makes!

"*Permaculture brings a sense of hope and responsibility. If we all took responsibility for our actions, then the world would be a very different place. When hope and responsibility are combined, they enable people to take a look inside their life, what they want to do, and how to move forward to make things different. Everything we do has a ripple effect, and if we respond with a sense of hope and responsibility then those ripples can be enormous and positive.*"
- **Looby Macnamara** www.loobymacnamara.com

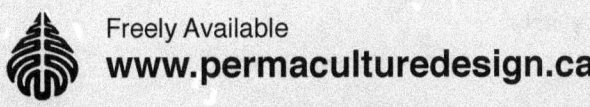

Freely Available
www.permaculturedesign.ca

# DESIGN FOR SOIL
## SHEET MULCHING AND HUGELKULTUR

### SHEET MULCHING
Layering newspaper, cardboard, hay, organic matter, manures, liquid fertilizer and other biodegradable materials is a great way to build new soil.

### HUGELKULTUR
A compost pile that can be turned into a garden while its still decomposing. The hugel, or mound, is made up of tougher materials like wood, blackberries, egg shells or fruit pits that do not break down at the same rate as the other composting materials. This can be used to make a productive living compost 'mound' bed.

Choose an area to build this bed. Cut plant growth down to just above the ground. Lay down newspaper and cardboard. Wet this well to begin decomposition and attract worms. Lay down heavy peaces of wood. Then a layer of lighter wood. Any brambles or vines can go next. Add some soil to kickstart the process. You could add biodynamic plants or preps at this stage too. Cover the pile with a layer of compost. Place a layer of soil on top. Plant with spike-root plants as these will help break down the wood. These are also ideal beds to grow biodynamic plants. Hugel beds hold water and are drought resistant. They also generate heat while decomposing making the gardens warmer in the winter for the first few years of its process. Eventually these beds will be totally broken down into kind garden soil.

"*I would like to see a world where there are wildlife corridors snaking right through all the suburbs, right into the centre of cities. This would allow animals to move through urban areas and children could have access to knowing the creatures of the woods. I would like to see a world where there is food resilience everywhere, from little window boxes and container gardens, to city parks with fruit, access to farms and wild spaces. I would like to see a world where every single person knows who they are, what they are here for, and is empowered to make their contribution. I would like to see a world where community overlaps and interweaves with community and where Earth care, People care and Fair Share is the norm on planet Earth so the ecosystem, and stratosphere are healthy places of abundance.*"
- **Robina McCurdy** www.earthcare-education.org

Freely Available
www.permaculturedesign.ca

PERMACULTURE WORKSHEET 037

# DESIGN FOR SOIL
## QUICK RETURN COMPOSTING

Gaiacraft loves the QR composting method innovated by Rudolf Steiner's student Maye Emily Bruce. What follows is gems of composting info mostly sourced from the excellent book 'Quick Return Compost Making : The Essence of the Sustainable Organic Garden' by Andrew Davenport.

Locally grown and harvested compost plants are slow dried and powdered with mortar and pestle. Honey is rubbed into dried sugar of milk. The powder lasts forever but is recommended to use within a year. The powder can also be added to the compost or mixed with rainwater to make a liquid feed, one pinch per wine bottle of water. Let sit for 24 hrs before adding to the compost and it lasts for one month. Store QR activator in glass in the dark. The QR method uses insulation like straw, sacking or fabric to hold in the heat and utilizes the Biodynamic Plants, some of the most powerful food-medicine plants on the planet.

**BIODYNAMIC PLANTS**
Incredibly, the compost plants have many different healing and nutritive qualities for people, animals, plants and soil organisms. They also have high mineral content and a long history of cultural significance. Biodynamics identifies these as some of the master medicine plants for Earth's ecology.

**Chamomile : Matricaria Chamomila**
- Sacred herb from Egypt and Pagan traditions
- High in potash, lime, phosphorus and sulphur
- Anti-inflammatory, anti-bacterial and anti-spasmodic
- Tea has a calming effect
- Restores and heals sick plants
- Increases production of essential oils in plants growing around it
- Biodynamics notes the affinity between chamomile and calcium, it is said to help guide the calcium forces in the breakdown of natural materials

**Dandelion : Leontodon Taraxacum**
- Used widely in Chinese medicine and European traditions
- High in potassium, iron, phosphorus, calcium, manganese, sodium, silicic acid and choline
- The roots contain inulin
- Good for treating gall bladder, stimulates digestive glands and liver issues
- Biodynamics notes this aids in the relationship between potassium and silica, allowing plants to draw on substances and forces from the entire district in which they live

Freely Available
www.permaculturedesign.ca

# DESIGN FOR SOIL
## QUICK RETURN COMPOSTING

**Valerian : Valeriana Officianalis**
- Long history of medicinal use in the west
- Cats and earthworms love it
- High in potash, lime, phosphorus and sulphur
- Promotes calmness and aids sleep, nervous tension, cramping, and also lowers blood pressure
- Famous in biodynamics for imparting warmth to the compost and for having readily accessible phosphorus content

**Yarrow : Achillea Millifolium**
- Used in Chinese and Western medicine for hundreds of years
- High in iron, lime, nitrates, potash, phosphorous, soda and sulphur
- Heals wounds, lowers fevers and blood pressure, stimulates digestion
- Biodynamics notes that its particularly good for replenishing soils

**Stinging Nettle : Urtica Dioica**
- Long history of medicinal use
- High in iron, magnesium, silicic acid, formic acid, carbonic acid, sodium, potassium, calcium, oil and vitamins A, B and C
- Blood cleanser, treating arthritis, lowering blood sugar, and encouraging breast milk production
- Helps neighbouring plants be more resistant to disease and increases content of their essential oils
- Stimulates the formation of humus in the soil
- Raises the heat of the compost pile
- Biodynamics claims it helps keep nitrogen content in soil from evaporating and enhances vegetative growth in plants

**Oak Bark : Quercus Robur**
- A sacred tree of the Pagan traditions
- High in potassium, lime and calcium
- Anti-inflammatory and antiseptic
- Biodynamics notes its special anti-fungal qualities in the compost
- Has a huge amount of implicate ecological connections

Freely Available
www.permaculturedesign.ca

# DESIGN FOR SOIL
## QUICK RETURN COMPOSTING

### QR ADDITIVES

**Comfrey : Symphytum officinale**
- Extremely high in potash, nitrogen, potassium, magnesium, calcium and iron
- Rich in protein but with low fibrous carbon so it breaks down quickly
- Great for making compost teas
- Heals bruises, burns, sores, sprains, broken bones
- Its leaves have same balanced NPK ratio as finished compost

**Horsetail : Equisetum arvense**
- Fungicide against mildew, rust and blackspot
- Discourages soil diseases
- Tea can be used to clean greenhouse
- Preventative medicinal tea for prostate in men
- Diuretic supporting kidney, bladder and strengthens bony tissue, hair and nails
- High in silica

**Raw Honey**
- Used for medicine for 4000 years
- Contains fructose, glucose, enzymes, sugars, gluconic acid, vitamins, minerals and amino acids
- Promotes growth of healing tissues and speeds up the healing process
- Anti-bacterial and antibiotic
- Draws in moisture from the air
- Preserves what you immerse inside it

**Sugar of Milk**
- Obtained from the whey of cow's milk by evaporation and purified by recrystallization
- Contains lactose, galactose and dextrose

**Quartz Crystal**
- Absorbs and radiates light
- Enhances photosynthesis
- Protects against some fungus

Freely Available
www.permaculturedesign.ca

**PERMACULTURE WORKSHEET 040**

# DESIGN FOR SOIL
## INTEGRATIVE WISDOM

*"Contemplating what we have learned and carefully designing our own next steps usually includes answering questions which were generated by the process and didn't even exist before. The drive to answer these questions can help us find our own niche. Permaculture design identifies many cycles in time and niches in space which we inevitably bring ourselves into. Where do I fit and how will I best serve? There is a logistical progression that we go through in permaculture that could include taking another Permaculture Design Course and ultimately leads to picking a place to practice. I try to inspire people to look at permaculture as a way of discovering their passion. What was it that sparked and got the most attention? Examine that. This could be something you may never even have even heard of before about mycology, carbon farming or over production. This passion can be something that you want to pursue. Permaculture design supports you to drive your own learning and be fueled by your own personal passion."*
- **Larry Santoyo** www.permacultureacademy.com


*"Permaculture is the Art of the Possible. It is the essence of creativity. As a discipline permaculture invites us to be wildly creative by building what are much closer to hunter gatherer systems than modern agriculture and accept that Yield is Unlimited. The arts, which is what people often think of when creativity is mentioned, have always been crucial in changing how people think. The arts are central to Permaculture's potential to be creative. Tony Buzan, the British psychologist, visionary and leader who invented MindMaps, talks about ten kinds of intelligence while admitting there are undoubtedly more. These ideas arose amongst psychologists in the 1990's and challenge the way our school and university educational systems work. Mainstream education mostly cater only to three kinds of intelligence: literacy, numeracy and social awareness. What about people who are great at caring, cooking, cleaning, or the mechanical skills of fixing things? Part of the challenge to letting the wonderfully creative aspects of Permaculture into your life is to unlearn the old restrictive attitudes that govern most of our educational systems and allow yourself to be wildly creative. Every design idea won't always work, but using continuous feedback loops we can adjust our design visions over time until they do. I worry about people who don't make mistakes, they are not trying to do anything new."*
- **Graham Bell** www.grahambell.org

Freely Available
www.permaculturedesign.ca

# DESIGN FOR SOIL
## QUICK RETURN COMPOSTING

### ALTERNATIVE QR COMPOSTING PLANTS

**Hollyhock - Althea rosea**
Iron, Soda, Potash, Phosphorus, Lime and Sulphur

**Black Walnut - Juglans nigra**
- High in Iron, Phosphorus, Potash, and Sulphur

**Alpine Strawberry - Fragaria vesca**
- High in Lime, Soda, and Phosphorus

**Yellow Dock - Rumex crispus**
- High in Iron and Sulphur

**Calendula - Calendula officinalis**
- High in Lime and Sulphur

**Sage - Salvia officinalis**
- High in Potash, Lime, and Soda

**Black Elderberry - Sambucus nigra or graveolens spp.**
- High in Iron, Potash, and Soda

**Chicory - Cichorium intybus**
- High in Iron, Potash, Lime, and Soda

Alternative species of Biodynamic Plants
English Oak - Quercus robber
Sessile Oak - Quercus petrel
Stinging Nettle - Urtica lyallii
Stinging Nettle - Urtica holosericea
Stinging Nettle - Urtica angustifolia
Valerian - Valeriana sambucifolia
German Chamomile - Matricaria recutita

Freely Available
www.permaculturedesign.ca

PERMACULTURE WORKSHEET 042

# DESIGN FOR SOIL
## SOIL SCIENCE

Utilize the power of remineralizing rock and crystal dust, biodynamic plants, kelp and cardboard in your compost in order to create a fertilizer charged with all the nutrients that plants eat. Here we review the elements needed for the healthy development of plants and examples of wild dynamic accumulator sources of these elements which you can add to your compost, vermiculture bin or hugelkultur. If you have room, these plants be grown in the area around your compost as they can tolerate some shade and poor soil.

A biodynamically infused soil will have all the elements that your plants need.

### PRIMARY ELEMENTS

**N - NITROGEN**
- Helps with plant growth and feeding microorganisms, is part of DNA, important in photosynthesis, needed to make plants green.
- Found in higher quantities in comfrey, stinging nettle, kelp, dandelion, yarrow, clover, lupine and chickweed.
- Lightning fixes nitrogen in soil.

**K - POTASSIUM**
- Helps with plant digestion, resistance to disease, cold, pests, develops buds, root development.
- Found in chamomile, chickweed, clover, stinging nettle, oak bark, yarrow, comfrey, dandelion, crabgrass, morning glory and kelp.

**P - PHOSPHOROUS**
- Helps with root growth, establishing young plants, photosynthesis, respiration, plant growth, and is an important mineral in DNA.
- Found in higher quantities in chamomile, chickweed, dandelion, yarrow, lamb's quarters and morning glory.

Freely Available
www.permaculturedesign.ca

# DESIGN FOR SOIL
## SOIL SCIENCE

### SECONDARY ELEMENTS

**Mg - MAGNESIUM**
- Helps with ripening and germination of seeds, and absorption of P, N and S.
- Found in higher quantities in comfrey, dandelion, horsetails, kelp, yarrow and stinging nettles.

**Ca - CALCIUM**
- Helps with development of root system, cell walls, ripening of fruits and seeds.
- Found in higher quantities in chamomile, comfrey, kelp, horsetail, stinging nettles, yarrow, morning glory and lamb's quarters.

**S - SULPHUR**
- Helps with chlorophyll production and helps plants absorb K, Ca and Mg.
- Found in higher quantities in stinging nettle, kelp, garlic, mullein, plantain and alfalfa.

### MINOR ELEMENTS

**Fe - IRON**
- Helps with chlorophyll production.
- Found in higher quantities in comfrey, dandelion, horsetail, kelp, yarrow and stinging nettles.

**B - BORON**
- Helps with overall plant health, formation of fruit and absorption of water.
- Found in higher quantities in cardboard, kelp and euphorbia.

**Mn - MANGANESE**
- Helps with seed germination and nitrogen assimilation.
- Found in higher quantities in chickweed, kelp, bracken fern, burdock, garlic and plantain.

**Mo - MOLYBDENUM**
- Helps with nitrogen assimilation and fixation.
- Found in higher quantities in clover and legumes.

Freely Available
www.permaculturedesign.ca

# DESIGN FOR SOIL
## SOIL SCIENCE

**Cl - CHLORINE**
- Helps stimulate photosynthesis.
- Found in higher quantities in kelp.

**Cu - COPPER**
- Helps activate enzymes and chlorophyll production.
- Found in higher quantities in dandelion, stinging nettle, valerian, yarrow, kelp, bracken fern and legumes.

**Zn - ZINC**
- Helps with protein synthesis, enzymes and growth hormones.
- Found in higher quantities in kelp, legumes, hay and Kentucky bluegrass.

**Si - SILICON**
- Helps with utilizing nitrogen and enzyme activation.
- Found in higher quantities in legumes.

**Ni - NICKEL**
- Helps with protection from disease and stress.
- Found in higher quantities in horsetail, borage, valerian and plantain.

**Co - COBALT**
- Helps with nitrogen fixing.
- Found in higher quantities in bracken fern, horsetail and vetches.

With a productive soil, a friendly neighbourhood of worms, and a conscious approach to waste management we can continue to evolve our approach to conscious living.

**Source Curriculum:** Bill Mollison, David Holmgren, Rosemary Morrow, Toby Hemenway, Maye Bruce, Robin Wheeler, Plants for a Future website www.pfaf.org

**Envoy:** Delvin Solkinson www.visionarypermaculture.com

**Foundational Work :** Kym Chi www.gigglingchitree.com

**Gaiacraft Workbook Editing Team :** Delvin Solkinson, Kym Chi, Annaliese Hordern, Tamara Griffiths, Jacob Aman, Tes Tesla, Niki Hammond

**Design :** Sijay James www.onbeyondmetamedia.com

Freely Available
www.permaculturedesign.ca

# DESIGN FOR SOIL
## SOIL SCIENCE

What is soil?
It's not simple. Soil is a complex mixture of several components, capable of supporting plant life. It originally formed by the weathering of the earth rock's. Typical soil contains approximately the following proportions of four main parts:

1. Minerals - about 45%
2. Water - about 25 %
3. Air - about 25%
4. Organic matter & living organisms - about 1 to 5%

The soil's minerals come from the underlying rocks. Plants need over a dozen mineral elements. Composition of typical soils would include: Organic matter, living portions, microbes, earthworms, etc., nitrogen, silicon dioxide, aluminum dioxide, iron oxide, calcium oxide, phosphate, potash, sulphur trioxide, manganese, zinc, copper, molybdenum, boron and chlorine.

The water in soils is necessary for plants, since plant tissue contains about 80 to 90 percent water. Water is especially important because it dissolves and carries nutrients and other materials inside the plant and in the soil. Air (oxygen) is essential for root growth, water and nutrient uptake, and for biological activity (soil life). Soil organic matter makes up less than 5% of the volume in most soils, but has an importance far out of proportion to it's amount. It plays major roles in the chemical, biological and physical aspects of soil fertility. Organic matter is not just one material it is a complex, dynamic mixture of substances.

Freely Available
www.permaculturedesign.ca

# DESIGN FOR SOIL
## SOIL SCIENCE

The science of renewable systems. It shows us what materials it is sustainable to use as well as how to effectively break those materials down into rich, healthy soil, mulch, and fertilizer. Our task is composting the old culture to provide energy and resources to build the new one.

In the Cool Climates, a simple cold compost is made by alternating layers of green material (nitrogen rich organic waste like grass clippings, kitchen waste, coffee grounds, tea bags, manure, garden weeds and other fresh vegetable matter) and brown material (carbon rich organic waste like leaves, dried grasses, or hay). Match the green and brown material for production of a heavy amendment or add more brown material for a higher organic matter soil. When you add any amount of new compost material, throw in some dead leaves, grass or newspaper to help with the decomposition process. Tougher materials like wood, blackberries, egg shells or fruit pits can be put into a different pile nearby the compost to be used for hugelkultur beds later. You may wish to avoid composting meat scraps, bones or any food (cooked or uncooked) that contains dairy, wheat, oil or fats as these materials rot instead of decomposing, creating stink and attracting rodents, flies and other pests. In order to have a steady supply of brown, carbonaceous material to use in layering the compost, collect of pile up brown materials like leaves and grass clippings next to the compost. The fall is the best time to gather this supply since there are so many dead leaves. If you are using manure, or have weed seeds in the compost, you may want to allow the compost to heat to at least 70 degrees celcius.

**Source Curriculum:** Farmer Dave Ryan
**Envoy:** Delvin Solkinson www.visionarypermaculture.com
**Foundational Work :** Kym Chi www.gigglingchitree.com
**Gaiacraft Workbook Editing Team :** Delvin Solkinson, Kym Chi, Annaliese Hordern, Tamara Griffiths, Jacob Aman, Tes Tesla, Niki Hammond
**Design :** Sijay James www.onbeyondmetamedia.com

Freely Available
www.permaculturedesign.ca

**PERMACULTURE WORKSHEET 047**

# DESIGN FOR SOIL
## SOIL HEALTH INDICATORS

### DANDELION
Indicates soils are acidic, cultivated, compacted, clay rich, low fertility, low in potassium and phosphorus
Soil functions : tap roots break up the soil, accumulates calcium, iron, copper, potassium and sulphur

### STINGING NETTLE
Indicates soils are acidic, heavily cultivated, compacted, clay
Soil functions : accumulates, nitrogen, copper, potassium and sulphur

### CLOVER
Indicates soils are heavy, acidic, low in nitrogen
Soil functions : fixes nitrogen, cover crop, accumulates potassium, and phosphorus

### CHICKWEED
Indicates soils are nitrogen rich, heavily cultivated, clay rich, fertile, wet or damp, alkaline
Soil functions : accumulates magnesium, manganese, potassium, phosphorus

### PLANTAIN
Indicates soils are clay, compacted, heavily cultivated, low fertility, acidic, poor drainage
Soil functions : accumulates silicon, sulphur, manganese and iron, when turned into soil, it reduces soil acidity

### THISTLE
Indicates soils are nitrogen rich, heavily cultivated, clay rich or dry depending on type of thistle
Soil functions : tap roots break up the soil, accumulates iron

  Freely Available
**www.permaculturedesign.ca**

**PERMACULTURE WORKSHEET 048**

# DESIGN FOR SOIL
## SOIL HEALTH INDICATORS

### SHEEP SORREL
Indicates soils are sandy, acidic, low fertility, especially potassium and phosphorus, low humus content
Soil functions: accumulates calcium, phosphorus and minerals that alkalinize the soil. Turning sorrel under makes minerals more available.

### DOCK
Indicates soils are wet or poorly drained, acidic
Soil functions : tap roots break up the soil, accumulates calcium, iron, phosphorus and potassium, helps soil structure

### MULLEIN
Indicates soils are: dry, crusty or compacted, low fertility
Soil functions : accumulates magnesium, sulphur and potassium

### QUACK GRASS
Indicates soils are: wet, clay rich, has a crusty surface.
Soil functions : helps control erosion on steep banks, accumulates silicon and potassium, contains certain insecticidal properties that cause nerve damage to slugs. Some people use finely chopped quack grass as a mulch to repel slugs (with the caution that too much of the mulch could damage plantings).

### VETCH
Indicates soils are: low fertility
Soil functions : fixes nitrogen, cover crop, accumulates phosphorus, potassium, copper and cobalt

### SCOTCH BROOM
Indicates soils are: low fertility, acidic soil
Soil functions : fixes nitrogen

Freely Available
www.permaculturedesign.ca

**PERMACULTURE WORKSHEET 049**

# DESIGN FOR SOIL
## NUTRIENT DEFICIENCY INDICATORS

### NITROGEN
General yellowing of older leaves (bottom of plant). The rest of the plant is often light green.

AMENDMENTS :
- Heavy mulching or cover cropping with clover, vetch or other legumes.
- Apply Seaweed extract.
- Apply compost tea of comfrey, stinging nettle, yarrow, dandelion and kelp.

### SULPHUR
Younger leaves turn yellow first, sometimes followed by older leaves.

AMENDMENTS:
- Compost tea of stinging nettle and kelp.
- Alfalfa hay as mulch .

### PHOSPHORUS
Leaf tips look burnt, followed by older leaves turning a dark green or reddish-purple.

AMENDMENTS:
- Apply wood ash.
- Sprinkle bone meal on soil.
- Apply compost tea of chamomile, dandelion and yarrow.
- Cover crop with chickweed.

### MAGNESIUM
Chlorosis or yellowing between leaf veins which stay green. Leaves may have a marbled appearance.

AMENDMENTS:
- Short term, use a light spray of epsom salts.
- Apply dolomite/ limestone.
- Apply compost tea of comfrey dandelion, horsetail, kelp and yarrow.

  Freely Available
www.permaculturedesign.ca

**PERMACULTURE WORKSHEET 050**

# DESIGN FOR SOIL
## NUTRIENT DEFICIENCY INDICATORS

### POTASSIUM
Older leaves may wilt, look scorched. Inter-veinal chlorosis begins at the base, scorching inward from leaf margins.

AMENDMENTS:
- Apply seaweed, manure, granite dust or greensand to the soil in fall.
- Apply hardwood ashes.
- Apply compost tea of chamomile, stinging nettle, oak bark, yarrow, comfrey, dandelion and kelp.
- Cover crop with chickweed or clove.

### CALCIUM
New leaves (top of plant) are distorted or irregularly shaped. Causes blossom-end rot.

AMENDMENTS:
- Apply compost tea of chamomile, comfrey, kelp, horsetail, stinging nettle and yarrow.

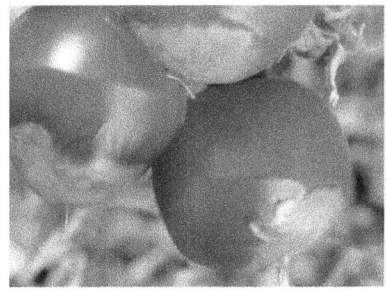

### MANGANESE
Yellowing occurs between the veins of young leaves. Pattern is not as distinct as with iron. Reduction in size of plant parts (leaves, shoots, fruit) generally. Dead spots or patches.

AMENDMENTS:
- Sprinkle dolomite/ limestone on soil - cover crop with chickweed.

### COPPER
Leaves are dark green with necrotic (dead) spots, plant is stunted, brown areas near the leaf tips.
AMENDMENTS:
- Compost tea of chamomile, horsetail, comfrey, stinging nettle, yarrow and kelp.
- Apply aged organic manure and compost tea.

Freely Available
www.permaculturedesign.ca

**PERMACULTURE WORKSHEET 051**

# DESIGN FOR SOIL
## NUTRIENT DEFICIENCY INDICATORS

### IRON
Yellowing occurs between the veins of young leaves.

AMENDMENTS:
- Add bone meal or blood meal organic amendments.
- Add 1-2 inches of compost in the spring every year.

### MOLYBDENUM
General yellowing of older leaves (bottom of plant). The rest of the plant is often light green. Heads can fail to form. Leaves will become thin, elongated and rippled.

AMENDMENTS:
- Add lime before planting - cover crop with clover.

### ZINC
Terminal leaves may be rosetted, and yellowing occurs between the veins of the new leaves.

AMENDMENTS:
- Apply aged organic manure.
- Compost tea of kelp.
- Mulch with hay.

### BORON
Terminal buds die, witches' brooms form. Youngest leaves may be red, bronze or scorched also small, thick or brittle. Stems stiff. Leaves highly tinted purple, brown and yellow.

AMENDMENTS:
- Apply household borax: 1 tbsp borax to 12 quarts of water. This will do 10 square feet of soil. Apply two times 2-3 weeks apart.
- Compost tea of kelp or mulch with cardboard.

Freely Available
www.permaculturedesign.ca

**PERMACULTURE WORKSHEET 052**

# DESIGN FOR SOIL
## INTEGRATIVE WISDOM

"Contemplating what we have learned and carefully designing our own next steps usually includes answering questions which were generated by the process and didn't even exist before. The drive to answer these questions can help us find our own niche. Permaculture design identifies many cycles in time and niches in space which we inevitably bring ourselves into. Where do I fit and how will I best serve? There is a logistical progression that we go through in permaculture that could include taking another Permaculture Design Course and ultimately leads to picking a place to practice. I try to inspire people to look at permaculture as a way of discovering their passion. What was it that sparked and got the most attention? Examine that. This could be something you may never even have even heard of before about mycology, carbon farming or over production. This passion can be something that you want to pursue. Permaculture design supports you to drive your own learning and be fueled by your own personal passion.

I believe that the single most important thing to do is learn how to do something. We need to learn by doing, even clumsily, even bad, even wrong, even destructive, because eventually we will get better. I want to see more people in our circles with scraped knuckles, missing digits and tales to tell. It's important you find that passion and pursue it at all costs. For example, the mechanical anything is going to be helpful in the future, thats the brilliant part of it!

In terms of a Permaculture Design Course, it's important to understand that as much as we want to have hands-on activities, as much as I want to give you the keys to the bulldozer, let me explain flow dynamics first. You tell me about the hydrologic cycle first and then I will be happy to let you have the keys to the D7 or even a shovel!. Lets first talk about soil and the way a plant fits in the landscape as well as the direction you plant it in before I give you that shovel. The hands-on part is going to be the easy part. The decision making that goes into where to plant something, what to plant, what time of year, is what I want you to know, that's what I want you to carry with you when you visit faraway lands."
- **Larry Santoyo** www.permacultureacademy.com

**Source Curriculum:** Weeds and What They Tell Us - Ehrenfried E Pfeiffer
**Envoy:** Delvin Solkinson www.visionarypermaculture.com
**Foundational Work :** Kym Chi www.gigglingchitree.com
**Gaiacraft Workbook Editing Team :** Delvin Solkinson, Kym Chi, Annaliese Hordern, Tamara Griffiths, Jacob Aman, Tes Tesla, Niki Hammond
**Design :** Sijay James www.onbeyondmetamedia.com

Freely Available
www.permaculturedesign.ca

**PERMACULTURE WORKSHEET 053**

# DESIGN FOR TREES
## FACTS AND FUNCTIONS

**EARTH**
- Feeds soil with captured nutrients and mulch
- Builds soil with biomass
- Sinks carbon
- Provide habitat for countless insects, organisms, animals and plants
- Can be nitrogen fixing and bioaccumulating
- Insulates houses and structures
- Provides fuel and construction materials
- Teaches people how nature works
- Provides food, nesting materials, medicine and tools for people and animals
- Play a key part of forest guilds and the symbiotic community of life that dwell there
- Protects from climatological factors
- Trees infuse 85% of rainfall with nutrient from plant cells, salts, dust, minerals and organic matter which slowly drips to the ground
- Trees give back 25% of their mass as nutrient rich biomass each year
- 13 million hectares of forests are cleared annually
- Nearly half the world's species of plants, animals and microorganisms will be destroyed or severely threatened over the next 1/4 century due to deforestation
- We are losing 137 plant, animal and insect species every single day due to deforestation
- On average each person uses two trees a day of wood their whole lives
- Ensure tree products last as long as the tree takes to grow
- The most rot resistant trees in cool climates are osage orange, cedar, black locust, pacific yew and red mulberry

"The next step after a Permaculture Design Course is practice. You have heard the words, seen the diagrams and gotten a taste of what permaculture is all about, now you've got to practice it. The practice can be as simple as having a container garden for lettuce and carrots outside on your patio, or it can be as complex as you want. Doing it is the main thing. Take the permaculture lesson and use it."
- **Scott Pittman** www.permaculture.org

Freely Available
www.permaculturedesign.ca

**PERMACULTURE WORKSHEET 054**

# DESIGN FOR TREES
## FACTS AND FUNCTIONS

### AIR
- Collect nutrient carried by wind and rain
- Cleanse and oxygenate air
- Dehumidify air in wet tropic climates
- Humidifies air in dry climates
- Deflects, channels or blocks wind
- Indicates wind factors
- Filters disease and weed seeds from wind
- A single mature tree can absorb carbon dioxide at a rate of 22.7 kg/ year (48 lbs) and release enough oxygen back into the atmosphere to support 2 human beings
- One acre of trees annually consumes the amount of CO2 equivalent to that produced by driving an average car for 41,483 km (26,000 miles)
- That same acre of trees also produces enough oxygen for 18 people to breathe for a year
- A 100 foot tree, 18" diameter at its base, produces 2721.5kg (6000lbs) of oxygen
- 60% of wind is forced up over the trees, then forms and falls as Eckman spirals. Trees can cause the moisture to drop because of the upward, forced spiralling of the wind. Rain is caused by these spirals if there is any moisture in the air

### FIRE
- Creates suntraps, heat sinks and cold sinks
- Turns light into chemical energy through photosynthesis
- Light colored bark and leaves reflect light through the forest
- Dark colored leaves and bark turns light to heat

"When we design, we are always building for future floods, future fires, future droughts, and planting a tree a few inches tall that will be future forest giants, throw future shadows. Future populations will need future soils and forest resources, shelter, security. So somebody needs to range ahead in time, scout out the next century. We are not daydreaming. We are time scouts. Finding places now for what will be needed then."
- **Bill Mollison**, Travels in Dreams

Freely Available
www.permaculturedesign.ca

**PERMACULTURE WORKSHEET 055**

# DESIGN FOR TREES
## FACTS AND FUNCTIONS

**WATER**
- Purify water
- Cause condensation (may exceed annual rainfall)
- Slow down runoff by absorbing water and causing a drip effect
- Evaporation during hot days cools air
- Condensation during cool nights warms air
- Pump water from the soil into air via transpiration
- Transpiration causes cloud cover and rainfall
- Rain seeding by putting particulate into the airstream
- Collect frost which melts and goes into the earth, increasing groundwater
- Slows snowmelt for longer release of water in spring thaw
- Biomass of trees holds nutrients and water
- Increase groundwater while keeping water table low
- Reduce ground evaporation and erosion
- Moisture is condensed at night on trees because it is relatively cooler than the air or wind
- 60% of inland water comes from forest transpiration
- Trees put more water into streams and lakes than rainfall due to capturing condensed moisture
- Ocean evaporation comes over land: 15% as rainfall, 85% as condensation
- Forests intercept 10 - 15 % of rainfall in the canopy
- Precipitation can be reduced up to 80% by deforestation
- Trees return 75% of precipitation to the air

"The roots of permaculture are two-fold, firstly there is our concern for the degradation of healthy habitat for life on earth, and secondly, there is an emerging hope that we can build a more functional, beautiful and individually constructive future for all people.

The easiest way to start is to look inwards, build your observation skills, listen to your body and respond. From this strong core we can become a peace-maker and a producer instead of a consumer. We can work delicately with the beautiful connections that surround us.

Permaculture (the search for a truly permaculture culture) will always be a human endeavour because we have an innate ability to create leaders in times of oppression."
- **April Sampson-Kelly** www.permaculturevisions.com

Freely Available
**www.permaculturedesign.ca**

PERMACULTURE WORKSHEET 056

# DESIGN FOR TREES
## STRATEGIES

**DEFORESTATION CAUSES**
- Habitat destruction
- Lower water table
- Less rainfall and alters localized weather patterns
- Soil erosion, depletes and degrades soil quality
- Displaces cultural connection to place

**STRATEGIES**
- Plant contour forests on slopes steeper than 15 degrees
- Ideally, 30% of land should be forested
- Use hedges to protect areas 5 times their height
- Food Forestry
- Windbreaks
- Fire Breaks
- Fedges
- Wildlife corridors
- Alley Cropping

"*The best way for an individual to practice permaculture is to do it wherever one is. If it is an urban lot then put in a small garden and perhaps a tree or two, if one has no land then help organize a community garden. I believe that ultimately one has to find one's community of friends and then grow with that community into a regenerative community.*"
- **Scott Pittman** www.permaculture.org

Freely Available
www.permaculturedesign.ca

**PERMACULTURE WORKSHEET** 057

# DESIGN FOR TREES
## NATURAL SUCCESSION MODELLING

- Identifying stages of succession as design considerations.
- When and where are we in the sequence of natural succession or human negative impact?
- Locate ourselves in the succession process.
- We have an opportunity to fast track, slow down or pause succession by intervening at the right time.

Successional changes in forest gardens over 10 years
- From all full sun plants to a dappled understory
- From plants vulnerable to weather to sheltered microclimates
- From highest production in lower layers to highest production in upper layers
- From needing imports of soil and mulch to being self sustaining

Successional changes in a forest. At each new stage, new plants join the life guild.
1-5 years after clearcut
- Pioneering plants including annual ground covers, weeds, and grass as well as perennial herbs and grasses
5-20 years a new ecosystem is forming
- Shrubs and woody plants
20 - 80 years grows an immature ecosystem
- Young wild trees
80 + years is a mature ecosystem
- Overstory canopy drops biomass and smaller plants and trees may begin to die off
500+ years is an ancient ecosystem
- Stabilized forest that grows to climax by 1000 years

**Conventional Farm** : annual plants clearcut and harvested every year, low biomass, low diversity, non-living mineral source of nutrient, low organic matter, few microclimates, low productivity, damaged by weather, rain, wind, sun and climate. Farm stays in the very beginning stage of succession.

**Forest** : perennial plants, high biomass, diversity and organic matter, many microclimates, biological source of nutrient (plants, animals and humus), complex niches, many symbiotic relationships and partnerships, high productivity, enhanced by weather, rain, wind, sun, climate.

**Permaculture Farm** : Perennial forest gardening. High productivity but we just harvest a small amount in order to allow it to reach increasingly climax states in the succession process. Acts like a highly productive forest system of mixed perennials and annuals.

Freely Available
www.permaculturedesign.ca

# DESIGN FOR TREES
## FOOD MICRO-FOREST GARDEN

**ALABASTER TERRACE IN THE HEART GARDENS**

This hearty native perennial foodscape fulfills beauty and ecological function while addressing pressing issues around food security for our uniquely conscious rainforest village. Celebrating the food and culture of the Coastal First Peoples, it reflects a diversity of relationships between plants, animals and people. This is part of a Roberts Creek Village Repair initiative to create place for people to gather, learn, share and help build a relocalized and resilient community future. As people walk, pedal or drive down the road into the village centre they will enter into beautiful gardens. Following the red brick path next to Heart of the Creek takes people and pets through shades of seasonal color and delicious snack foods they can eat as they pass by. Signage will help people learn about the plants, their functions and edibility as well as their place within the Cultures of the Land. The forest garden dapples the transition from bustling village centre to the cement road and its traffic. On the other side of the red brick path is the Heart Gardens plant community of 250 species of perennial food including 150 species of native perennials used traditionally as food-medicine plants. Featured in this Food Micro-Forest are keystone food producing native trees which reflect their cousins across the street (also crab apples and hazelnuts). Under the trees are sentinel plants to break up the soil and prevent crowding from other plants while attracting birds, bees and butterflies. Between the trees are native berry bushes feeding people and attracting birds, below which is an edible ground cover as a living mulch and beneficial insect attractor. This is the start of the guild and its main components, other small herbaceous level plants will be added later to enhance diversity and ecological function.

*"If you have a dysfunctional institution, don't try to change it. Rather, determine what that institution was suppose to deliver and design a better system to actually deliver that purpose or service. If you have done this correctly, then people will come to you. The old institution will eventually wither and die"*
- **Bill Mollison** www.tagari.com

Freely Available
www.permaculturedesign.ca

# DESIGN FOR TREES
## FOOD MICRO-FOREST GARDEN

**SEASONAL INTEREST**
Winter : January, February, March
Growth : Hazelnut Catkins, Sweet Gale
Berries : Bearberries
Harvests : Greenery and Foliage

Spring : April May June
Flowers : Crab Apples, Hazelnuts, Soopolallie, Sweet Gale, Serviceberry, Strawberries, April Black Lily, May Chocolate Lily, June Camas
Harvests : Hazel Nuts

Summer : July, August, September
Flowers : Labrador Tea, Kinnickinnick, Nodding Onion, Camas, July Tiger Lily
Harvests : Crab Apples, Buffalo Berries, Serviceberries, Strawberries

Autumn : October, November, December
Flowers : Deciduous leaves provide the color
Harvests : Dogwood Berries, Bearberries
Foliage : Serviceberry changes colors.

**FUNCTIONS**
Edibility: Fruit, Berries, Nuts, Oil, Leaves, Roots, Starch, Inulin, Vitamin C, Teas
Traditional Ethnobotany : Medicines for heart complaints, tooth pain, intestinal disorders, eyes, organs and skin, digestion, and blood pressure. Includes female tonic, and healers of stomachic issues, diarrhea, dysentery, kidney stones, respiration, colds, coughs and fevers. Produces a smoking blend tobacco substitute and series of vitalizing teas.
Tool making: Hard wood for tools like bows, tool handles, pegs and fish hooks, digging sticks, cooking and drying racks, building poles, and arrows. There is pliable materials for basketry, as well as rope and string. The guild also provides wax for burning, essential oil perfume and insect repellants. Blue, red and yellow Dye is traditionally made from plants in this community.
Beneficial Ecological Function: Pollinators, nitrogen fixers, living mulch, sentinel plants, insectary plants, beneficial animal and insect attractors, native habitat, repels pests and rodents, kills mosquitos and fleas.
Food for: Red squirrels, chipmunks, birds, bees, butterflies, honeybees.
Attracts birds: Hummingbirds, song birds, grouse, waxwings, sapsuckers, woodpeckers, towhees, sparrows, grosbeaks, robins and countless others.

Freely Available
www.permaculturedesign.ca

**PERMACULTURE WORKSHEET 060**

# DESIGN FOR TREES
## FOOD MICRO-FOREST GARDEN

**SHRUBS**

### Pacific Crab Apple - Malus fusca
Bloom Time: (Spring) May June
Edibility: Keystone plant of the Coastal First Peoples. Apples are easy to store for long periods of time.
Medicine: For the eyes, organs and skin.
Tool making: Hard wood for tools like bows, handles, pegs and fish hooks.
Beneficial Ecological Function: Universal Pollinator for Apples. Attracts beneficial insects. Food for birds.
Water: Drought tolerant.
Soil: Hearty and tolerant.
Sun: Sun - Part Shade.

### Beaked Hazelnut - Corylus cornuta
Bloom Time: Catkins (Winter) February-March
Flowers (Spring) April-May
Edibility: Nutritious seeds store for a year. The only native plant source for nuts and oil
Traditional Medicine: heart complaints, tooth pain and intestinal disorders.
Tool making: Basketry, arrows, blue dye, rope and string.
Beneficial Ecological Function: Nuts are eaten by native squirrels and birds.
Water: Drought tolerant.
Soil: Hearty and tolerant.
Sun: Semi-shade to sun.

### Creek Dogwood - Cornus sericea
Bloom Time: Flowers (Summer) May to July Berries (Autumn) October
Edibility: Berries eaten by interior peoples but not preferred.
Traditional Medicine: Bark extract was used for treating coughs and fevers, and tea brewed from roots and stems was used to prevent and treat malaria. A tonic plant. Some tribes smoked the inner layers of the bark as a tobacco substitute.
Tool making: Source of red dyes. Fibre for rope and basketry. Cooking and drying racks.
Beneficial Ecological Function: Berries are a preferred food and nesting site of many songbirds, particularly during fall migration. Flowers are an important source of pollen for honey bees. Food for red squirrels and chipmunks.
Water : Prefers moist conditions.
Soil: Commonly occurs on moist, organic soils, but grows in a wide range of soil types.
Sun: Sun and Shade tolerant.

  Freely Available
www.permaculturedesign.ca

**PERMACULTURE WORKSHEET 061**

# DESIGN FOR TREES
## FOOD MICRO-FOREST GARDEN

**Serviceberry - Amelanchier alnifolia**
Bloom Time: Flowers (Summer) April and May Foliage (Autumn)
Edibility: Berries were an important plant food used by the First Peoples. Pemmican was made by pounding dried service berries with dried meat.
Traditional Medicine: Stomachic, fevers, flu.
Tool making: Arrow shafts, digging sticks and building poles were made from the hard, straightgrained wood. Slat armor and shield.
Beneficial Ecological Function: Numerous birds eat the fleshy fruits and find shelter among the branches. This species is able to re-sprout after fire. A great source of pollen and nectar for bees and butterflies.
Tool Making : Rope and tool handles.
Water: Likes moist.
Soil: Occurs on a variety of well- drained soils.
Sun: Semi-shade or sun.

## GROUND COVER

**Coastal Strawberry - Fragaria chiloensis**
Bloom Time: Flower (Spring) April May Fruit (Summer) June July
Edibility: Berries and leaf tea.
Traditional Medicine: female tonic, burns, diarrhea.
Tool making: Woven headbands.
Beneficial Ecological Function: Living mulch, attracts butterflies, bees and birds.
Water: Drought tolerant.
Soil: Soil tolerant.
Sun: Sun or shade.

**Woodland Strawberry - Fragaria virginiana**
Bloom Time: Flower (Spring) April May Fruit (Summer) June July
Edibility: Berries and leaf tea high in vitamin c.
Traditional Medicine: female tonic, burns, diarrhea.
Tool making: Fruits help clean teeth.
Beneficial Ecological Function: Living mulch, attracts butterflies and bees.
Water: Drought tolerant.
Soil: Soil tolerant.
Sun: Sun or shade.

Freely Available
www.permaculturedesign.ca

# DESIGN FOR TREES
## FOOD MICRO-FOREST GARDEN

**Mountain Strawberry - Fragaria vesca**
Bloom Time: Flower (Spring) April May Fruit (Summer) June July
Edibility: Berries and leaf tea.
Traditional Medicine: dysentery.
Tool making: Woven headbands.
Beneficial Ecological Function: Living mulch, attracts butterflies and bees.
Water: Drought tolerant.
Soil: Soil tolerant.
Sun: Sun or shade.

**Kinnickinnick - Arctostaphylos uva-ursi**
Bloom Time: May to June
Edibility: Fruit
Traditional Medicine: The dried leaves were smoked as a tobacco substitute by combining dried leaves with the dried inner-bark of red osier dog wood. urinary infections, mouth wash.
Tool making: Dye, waterproofing.
Beneficial Ecological Function: The berries are eaten by various birds.
Water: Grows in areas with 8-45 inches of annual precipitation.
Soil: Occurs on a variety of soil types including sandy, acidic, and well- drained to excessively-drained soils.
Sun: Full Shade and Semi-Shade or sun.

## ROOTS

**Nodding Onion - Allium cernuum**
Bloom Time: (Summer) June July
Edibility: Flowers, leaves, roots, contains inulin.
Traditional Medicine: kidney stones, respiration, colds, sore throats.
Beneficial Ecological Function: Attracts hummingbirds, bees and butterflies, repels insect and rodent pests, insect repellant for humans, sentinel plants to prevent weed crowding.
Water: Drought tolerant.
Soil: Soil tolerant.
Sun: Part sun to sun.

Freely Available
www.permaculturedesign.ca

# DESIGN FOR TREES
## FOOD MICRO-FOREST GARDEN

**Common Camas - Camassia quamash**
Bloom Time: (Summer) May June
Edibility: Nutritious tuber, contains inulin.
Traditional Medicine: Childbirth.
Beneficial Ecological Function: Feeds bees and attracts butterflies, sentinel plants to prevent weed crowding.
Water: Likes moist.
Soil: Soil tolerant.
Sun: Sun or shade.

**Black Lily - Fritillaria camchatcensis**
Bloom Time: (Spring) May
Edibility: Bulb eaten as a Staple Food or used to make flour.
Beneficial Ecological Function: Sentinel plants to prevent weed crowding.
Water: Likes moist.
Soil: Soil tolerant.
Sun: Sun or shade.

**Chocolate Lily - Fritillaria lanceolata**
Bloom Time: (Spring) April May
Edibility: High starch bulb was a staple food for Coastal First Peoples.
Beneficial Ecological Function: sentinel plants to prevent weed crowding.
Water: Likes moist.
Soil: Soil tolerant.
Sun: Sun or shade.

**Source Curriculum:** Bill Mollison, David Holmgren, Rosemary Morrow, Toby Hemenway, Robin Clayfield, Larry Santoyo, Michael Becker, Looby Macnamara, Scott Pittman, Geoff Lawton, Robyn Francis, Mark Lakeman, Patricia Michael, Starhawk, Bullock Brothers, Tom Ward, Jude Hobbs

**Envoy:** Delvin Solkinson www.visionarypermaculture.com

**Foundational Work :** Kym Chi www.gigglingchitree.com

**Gaiacraft Workbook Editing Team :** Delvin Solkinson, Kym Chi, Annaliese Hordern, Tamara Griffiths, Jacob Aman, Tes Tesla, Niki Hammond

**Design :** Sijay James www.onbeyondmetamedia.com

Freely Available
www.permaculturedesign.ca

# DESIGN FOR ANIMALS
## INTEGRATIVE FARMING

Integrating wild and domestic animals into our systems brings fertility and abundance and allows us to work with nature to create effective, efficient and ethical systems.

### FACTS
- 1/3 of human food is reliant on bees in some way.
- Animal livestock covers 45% of the earth's total land.
- 2-5 acres of land are used per head of cattle.
- Agricultural practices in industrial scale livestock trade is the leading cause of habitat destruction, species decline and water pollution.
- As many as 2.7 trillion marine animals are pulled from the ocean each year.
- For every 1 pound of fish caught, up to 5 pounds of unintended marine species are caught and discarded back to the ocean as bycatch
- Up to 137 plant, animal and insect species are lost every day due to rainforest destruction
- Using industrial agriculture
1.5 acres can produce 37,000 pounds of plant-based food
1.5 acres can produce 375 pounds of meat

### STRATEGIES
- Ensure suitable local conditions
- Establish the system then introduce the animals
- Quarantine all new animals
- Ensure sustainable water access
- Increase onsite food production of animal feed
- Design for forage
- Consider welfare, needs and protection
- Research stocking rates and breeding habits
- Build appropriate fencing
- Learn how to work with manure and outputs
- Reduce impact to the natural ecology
- Integrated poultry systems and chicken tractors
- Pasture Cropping
- Rotational Grazing
- Fodder along fence edges

Freely Available
www.permaculturedesign.ca

# DESIGN FOR ANIMALS
## INTEGRATIVE FARMING

### PESTS
- Pest are indicators that something is out of balance
- Pests are a natural part of life and may require deterring or elimination
- Aim to keep pests at a level with minimal or acceptable damage

### CAUSES OF PEST
- Monocultures
- Pesticides
- Warmer climate
- Increased humidity
- Drought
- Loss of natural habitat
- Lack of predators

### INTEGRATED PEST MANAGEMENT
Control pests by creating food and habitat for natural predators

### COMMON PESTS
- Mosquitos
- Aphids
- Mice and rats
- Slugs
- Skunks
- Raccoons
- Deer
- Bears
- Humans

Freely Available
www.permaculturedesign.ca

# DESIGN FOR ANIMALS
## INTEGRATIVE FARMING

### COMMON PREDATORS
- Dogs
- Cats
- Wasps
- Ladybugs
- Ducks
- Geese
- Guinea fowl
- Chickens
- Hawks, eagles, ravens and other birds
- Wolves
- Coyotes

### COMMON BENEFICIALS
- Butterflies
- Frogs
- Spiders
- Mason bees
- Hummingbirds
- Garter snakes
- Beavers

### DESIGN TECHNIQUES
- Integrated poultry systems and chicken tractors
- Pasture Cropping
- Rotational Grazing
- Fodder along fence edges

**Source Curriculum:** Bill Mollison, David Holmgren, Rosemary Morrow, Toby Hemenway, Robin Clayfield, Larry Santoyo, Michael Becker, Looby Macnamara, Scott Pittman, Geoff Lawton, Robyn Francis, Mark Lakeman, Patricia Michael, Starhawk, Bullock Brothers, Tom Ward, Jude Hobbs

**Envoy:** Delvin Solkinson www.visionarypermaculture.com

**Foundational Work :** Kym Chi www.gigglingchitree.com

**Gaiacraft Workbook Editing Team :** Delvin Solkinson, Kym Chi, Annaliese Hordern, Tamara Griffiths, Jacob Aman, Tes Tesla, Niki Hammond

**Design :** Sijay James www.onbeyondmetamedia.com

Freely Available
www.permaculturedesign.ca

**PERMACULTURE WORKSHEET 067**

# DESIGN FOR ANIMALS
## COOL CLIMATE CHICKEN FODDER

**Lance's List of Great Fodder plants for Chooks**

By relocalizing your chicken feed you can create a closed loop saving time, energy and money while reducing your ecological footprint and feeding your chickens more nutritious food. Here are some great chicken fodder plants for the Cool Climates.

**TREES**
Mulberry (16% protein)
Mountain Ash / Rowan
Holly
Oak Acorns (cracked)
Maple Tree keys
Hawthorn
Persimmon (pigs favourite)
Fruit
Privet
Creeping Raspberry and Blackberry
Grapes
Rosehips
Goji
Sea Buckthorn
Kiwi
Weeds
Purslane
Duckweed
Chickweed

Freely Available
www.permaculturedesign.ca

PERMACULTURE WORKSHEET 068

# DESIGN FOR ANIMALS
## COOL CLIMATE CHICKEN FODDER

**PLANTS**
Comfrey (Russian Bocking 4)
Siberian Pea Shrub
Tagasaste
Alfalfa
Day Lily
Pumpkins and Squashes
Sunflower
Kudzu
Cow Peas
Fodder beets
Turnips
Jerusalem Artichoke
Clover (White Dutch is best)
Lambs Quarters
Dandelion
Golden Dock
Kelp
Bush Clover
Perennial Grains including Rye, Sorghum, Quinoa, Amaranth. These won't work well for a free range system but great for fodder feed.

**MEAT**
Meal Worms
Slugs (feed in small pieces at first)
Black Solider Fly Larva (42% protein, 35% fat)
Mice

**Source Curriculum:** Lance Wildwood

**Envoy:** Delvin Solkinson www.visionarypermaculture.com

**Foundational Work :** Kym Chi www.gigglingchitree.com

**Gaiacraft Workbook Editing Team :** Delvin Solkinson, Kym Chi, Annaliese Hordern, Tamara Griffiths, Jacob Aman, Tes Tesla, Niki Hammond

**Design :** Sijay James www.onbeyondmetamedia.com

Freely Available
www.permaculturedesign.ca

# DESIGN FOR ANIMALS
## DEEP ECOLOGY

Deep ecology is a larger perspective on the role and place of people in the evolutionary history life on the planet. This is a remix of an original story told by John Seed and Joanna Macy. Here we can think about our more-than-human world from a more-than-human perspective. The intention is to inspire imagination, explore evolution, and create a legacy of planetary stewardship.

Cradled in the 14 billion year history of the Milky Way Galaxy, our solar system evolved from a free horizon of cosmic clouds and galactic gasses. 4 billion years ago, when our planet began to cool, and the ocean of molecular soup was potentized by electric energy, the first cell was borne. We all trace our genetic and epigenetic lineage to this single event, as does every cell of every living thing on Earth. Every single cell in our bodies is a direct descendent in an unbroken chain from that original cell. In this way we are intimately, energetically and physically related to all living things.

The first one celled organisms evolved into forms of bacteria, some of which created the oxygen that began to form the biosphere. 1 billion years ago the first multicellular organisms evolved as algae and then seaweed, creating an atmosphere that killed much of the bacteria and made it possible for further developments of plant life. 600 million years ago simple water creatures like flatworms, jellyfish and sponges began to inhabit the world ocean. During this time there was a vast ice age on the earth wiping out many prehistoric gene pools. 550 million years ago came fungi who began to create soil. 500 million years ago came fish, the first vertebrates to emerge from the evolutionary chain of being. 25 million years later green plants had moved onto the land and began to cultivate the soil strata. Millipedes and centipedes were amongst the first animals to travel across the land, cultivating dry habitat around 450 million years ago. Spiders and scorpions developed soon after and early, wingless insects like silverfish could be seen on the newly greening landscapes. 300 million years ago the Earths geography began to develop as a PanGaian supercontinent known as Pangea. This began a period of unbridled evolution. Insects developed wings and 2 foot long dragonflies could be seen flying through forests of ferns, moss and horsetail. During this time, seed bearing plants are sweeping across the fertile lands, and amphibians beginning to emerge. 250 million years ago came reptiles and the great dinosaurs. It was an age of monsters and mayhem in a vast civilization of wild prehistoric animals. During the next period of 50 million years there are two major extinction events which decimated the Earths diverse population. About 180 million years ago Pangaia began to split apart and continents formed, these were populated with dinosaurs and increasingly forested landscapes. 130 million years ago pollen containing flowers began to form and beautiful new colors come to our Gardenic Earth.

Freely Available
www.permaculturedesign.ca

**PERMACULTURE WORKSHEET 070**

# DESIGN FOR ANIMALS
## DEEP ECOLOGY

During this time the first proto-mammals begin to develop. 65 million years ago a huge meteor strikes the Earth killing most of the dinosaurs and made space for mammalian development. A mere 55 million years ago the first primates began to appear, changing into our first ancestors over a 40 million year process. Major climatological changes on the planet saw the great rainforests recede and turn to grasslands. Tribal Ape cultures began to develop. It was only a mere 100,000 years ago that the Neanderthal began the evolutionary ascent into modern humanity.

The earliest cave paintings show humans communicating with art 32,000 years ago marking the beginning of recorded human history. This evolutionary storyline shows that our roots reach deep. To this day the first few weeks of human embryonic development is identical to the embryonic development of all animals, reptiles and fish. We are all connected.

Being responsible stewards of the Earth means taking to heart the current planetary healing crisis. What are the long term consequences of GMO seeds, mono - cropping, fish farming, deforestation, desertification, waste mismanagement, urbanization, chemical fertilizers, terminator seeds, acid rain, global warming, fossil fuel depletion, species extinction, cultural appropriation and warfare? Canada hosts some of the last whooping cranes, peregrine falcons, burrowing owls and beluga whales. Through the toxic destruction of their natural habitats, and introduction of foreign species into the eco-system, these beautiful creatures are now on the endangered species list. What endangered species are in your local area? Canada has seen the total extinction of labrador ducks, passenger pigeons, and the flightless relatives of the penguins, the great auks. What animals from your area are now extinct? Since everything is connected, humanity must revision the way it relates to our process of being in the world. Remember that humanity is in transition, here to grow our awareness, refine the way we build human communities, and evolve our relationship to the World Ecology. Remain grateful that our ecosystem is still intact and hosts tens of thousands of species of plants, animals, insects and fungi. There is a whole world to save and its not too late to play an active role in this most ethical of actions. Take decisive steps to revitalizing and protecting the web of life into which everything is woven.

**Source Curriculum:** John Seed www.johnseed.net, Joanna Macy www.joannamacy.net

**Envoy:** Delvin Solkinson www.visionarypermaculture.com

**Foundational Work :** Kym Chi www.gigglingchitree.com

**Gaiacraft Workbook Editing Team :** Delvin Solkinson, Kym Chi, Annaliese Hordern, Tamara Griffiths, Jacob Aman, Tes Tesla, Niki Hammond

**Design :** Sijay James www.onbeyondmetamedia.com

Freely Available
**www.permaculturedesign.ca**

# DESIGN FOR WATER
## LIFE SOURCE

Water is the source of life.
It is a universal solvent, dissolving more substances then any other liquid.

**FACTS**
- 60% of the wetlands have been destroyed in the past 100 years
- Up to 40% of rainforest in forested areas is caused by the forest itself
- 70% of our earths surface is water
93.8% is ocean water
2.5% is fresh water
0.375% is accessible to humans
0.3% of water is in Lakes & ponds
0.06% is from soil moisture & forests
0.03% is in rivers
0.035% is in the atmosphere
- Average water use
in wealthy countries is 2,400 litres a week
in in developing world 225 litres a week
- The average north american uses more than 227 litres
of water per day 26 % by toilet flushing, 17% by showering, 15% from taps, 22% by clothes washer, 14% by sub surface leaks, 5% from other uses
- Industrial agriculture uses
677 litres of water to grow 1 pound of wheat
1,198 litres of water to grow 1 pound of rice
99 litres of water to grow one apple
5.2 million litres of water to raise one large cow
200 litres of water to produce 1 litre of bottled water
- Source of water in the environment
13 percent of precipitation is rain
86 percent of precipitation is from condensation harvested from sea air, mists and fogs
85% of water use is from agriculture
7.5% of water use is from industry
7.5 % of water use by residential and a large percentage of that is lawns
- Hydrological cycle : water moves from the ocean to clouds to rain to filtering flows and back to ocean. There are many mini hydrologic cycles through tree and plant evapotranspiration
- Rain is formed over oceans from iodine particles
- Rain is formed over forests from particulate
- Websites of interest www.findaspring.com www.danielvitalis.com

Freely Available
www.permaculturedesign.ca

**PERMACULTURE WORKSHEET 072**

# DESIGN FOR WATER
## LIFE SOURCE

### CRISIS
Polluted water is toxifying the planet, lowering sperm counts and increasing miscarriages in humans it is caused by:
- Agriculture which pollutes groundwater
- Automobiles whose emissions pollute clouds
- Industry which pollutes air, soil and water
- Salinization which is caused by deforestation and rising of water tables coupled with increased evaporation due to agricultural watering
- Bottled water is taking water out of the hydrologic cycle and denying plants, animals and people from free water access

### STORAGE
- Cisterns, rain barrels, tanks, ponds, dams, swales, in soil, in vegetation and animals
- Roof catchment collection formula :
1 millimetre of rainfall on 1 square meter of roof will yield 1 litre of water.
10mm of rain on a 20 square meter roof will yield 200 litres of water.
- If annualizing rain yield based on rainfall figures multiply by 0.6 to allow for losses caused by evaporation etc.
- Metal roofs can add up to 500 litres a year in water on an average 20 x 18 meter roof from condensation

### CONSERVATION
- Native and drought resistant plant species
- Arrange plants by water needs (hydro-zoning)
- Dense planting
- Heavy mulching
- Replace lawns with useful ground covers and vegetation
- Use soil rich in organic matter
- Contour land with swales
- Harvest rain and dew
- Drip irrigation
- Hand watering or drip lines instead of sprinklers
- Low flush toilets or compost toilets
- Using grey and black water systems
- Low pressure shower heads
- Use buckets in the sink or shower
- Use an egg timer to take 4 minute showers

Freely Available
www.permaculturedesign.ca

# DESIGN FOR WATER
## LIFE SOURCE

**TREATMENT**
- Multiple types of filtration and water cleansing
- Aeration through flow forms and waterwheels
- Settling through reed beds and ponds, both anaerobic digesters and aerobic ponds
- Filtering by running water through sand, gravel or charcoal filters
- Biological cleansing with fish, bacteria, plankton or bioremediating plants
- Nature cleans water by oxygenating, vortexing, sun sterilizing, phytoremediation (plant filtration), particulate filtration, mimic this
- Effective ways of recycling and purifying waste water and flushing nutrients into your agriculture system

**STRATEGIES**
- Think of water as an important resource
- Reduce use before trying to save water to fulfill your needs
- Design for multiple sources and reserves
- Maximize living and organic ground cover to help slow evaporation
- Key goal is to preserve, protect and refill the aquifer
- When rehydrating land always start at the top of the hill or watershed
- Locate water storage at the highest point on the land for gravity feed
- Locate the design site in relation to the water shed
- Think of the watershed as a water spread
- Always plan for excessive rain events and design for the overflow pathways
- Plan for water distribution throughout the landscape, don't try to catch it all at the lowest point of elevation
- Create a community plan for water catchment
- Leave 15% of water storage as surface water, to help reduce risk of fire and buffer against climate change

**PRINCIPLES OF WATER**
- Rural : slow, spread, sink and store
- Urban : save it, store it, use it, reuse it, clean it, release it
- Channel water along the longest path (over the most distance), traveling as slowly as possible (over the most time), rubbing up to as many things as possible (with the most passive friction), to create the most fertility. It's less about the amount of water you have then it is about the amount of times you use it.

Freely Available
www.permaculturedesign.ca

**PERMACULTURE WORKSHEET 074**

# DESIGN FOR WATER
## TECHNIQUES

- Cleaning of creeks and rivers
- Restitution creek lines
- Restoration of remnant ecology
- Coastal Permaculture
- Permaculture for Delta peoples (1/3 of the world lives on deltas)
- Brackish and salt water systems, gardens and islands floated on reeds
- Use of macrophytes, water filtering edge species
- Do a water audit with the objective to save enough water that you can fulfill your needs all year
- Water in glass bottles that allow evaporation to get rid of ammonia and chlorine
- **Agro Plow or Yeomans Plow** : used for soil conditioning, dragged along contours to cut into soil and break things up, allows water into the soil and roots to go deeper, keeping soil aerated
- **Vertical Mulch** : cut channel into soil and put in straw, then plant into it
- **Net and Pan** : for existing orchards or individual trees, build a half sized saucer shaped berm that is level at the drip line on the downhill side of the tree, a small ditch connects overflow with diversion canals or pipes down to lower trees on a minimal angle so passage of water does not cause erosion
- **Blackwater** : pee down a pipe into pit full of gravel with a layer of coal and sand which is planted with bioremediators, the water overflows to a pond below where wind and sun can sterilize it, then trickles through stones downhill for oxygenation to a final pond used for irrigation and fire protection
- **Roof Collection** : Best is glass, photo voltaic, metal roof or shake roof
Asphalt tag roofing is only for sub-irrigation or swales (not for tanks), high in anaerobic bacteria and petroleum products
- **Galvanized roof** : hot dripped is full of cyanide, electric process is ok, but has alot of zinc, this means water is ok for drinking but not for irrigation (plants dont like zinc) beware paint chips that contain heavy metals (filter chips in settling tank)
- Rain tanks and cisterns vary in size and can be used for catching water from different sources, mainly from roofs. They should be level and raised for water pressure. When catching water from eavestroughs or downspouts, a first flush system is recommended

Freely Available
www.permaculturedesign.ca

PERMACULTURE WORKSHEET 075

# DESIGN FOR WATER
## TECHNIQUES

- **Wicking Beds** : Efficient self contained systems
Filter and hold water in gravel below the soil and water wicks up through organic matter to reach plant roots
Can be built in-ground or above ground, making them especially helpful for renters or homeowners who have limited growing space
Consist of a water proof membrane, piping or weeping tile, 9 inches of gravel and 13 inches of rich composted soil
- **Rain Garden** : Low cost/ low maintenance systems used for water capture and filtration
Typically built on a higher part of a property and connected to a downspout or grey water system
Created to be level with a berm on the down slope side
Planted with water loving/ water purifying species that are also often beneficial bird and insect attractors
Should hold water for up to 24 hrs for purification
- **Flow Forms** : Consist of a series of oval shaped containers that pour into one another from top to bottom on a slope or hill, typically a figure eight pattern
- **Curb Cuts** : Used in urban settings to capture and store run off water and irrigate planted systems along boulevards
Creates biodiversity in public urban areas and helps to reduce risk of flooding
- **Ponds** : Creates biodiversity and microclimates especially when edge is maximized
Used for aquaculture, providing food and nutrient
Recommended to have water purifying plants cover up to 30% of surface area and plant edges with reeds
- Prevent farm animals from accessing ponds with appropriate fencing
- **Reforestation** : Trees effectively condense water from the air at night and increases air humidity, cloud formation and rain
Tree roots also help reduce erosion during heavy rain/flooding events
- **Diversion drain** : Enables effective water harvesting and storage
Acts as a dependable system in emergencies
Recharges sand basins and swales
Dampens wild fires
Can be built on keyline systems or led into swales
Can be made of concrete or stone

Freely Available
www.permaculturedesign.ca

**PERMACULTURE WORKSHEET 076**

# DESIGN FOR WATER
## TECHNIQUES

### SWALE
- a level ditch on contour with planted downhill berm intended for catching overland flow and infiltrate into the ground to recharge the surrounding soils, plant root systems and aquifer
- Slope swale at 1-3 m vertical intervals, with swales of 2 m deep, and 3-5 m wide
- Gentle slope of less than 15 degrees can handle swales every 3 metres
- Downhill berm can have trees on it and/or just below it
- Make swales smaller and closer together in dry areas or larger and further apart in wet areas
- In clay conditions put swales closer together
- In sandy soil conditions put swales further apart
- On steeper slopes consider a bench or terracing to trap nutrient and slow water coming into the swale
- If in dry area you can plant the swale
- In wet area put in bench or terrace and plant the swale too
- Plant into swales starting with nitrogen fixing green cover crops and pioneers
- Indication of successful swale is recharged springs emerging at the bottom of the slope
- You can put small walls into the swale to keep water compartmentalized and not loose all water when swale is eroded
- Well designed swales hold water for up to three days
- Reduces mosquitoes
- Swales help with soil catchment and creation
- www.swalecalculator.com

### KEY LINE DESIGN
Off contour water storage and flow systems
Begins uphill with a study of the contours, then dams are built up high, protected with plantings, and water is distributed by gravity
Allows for controlled flood irrigation
Provides quick regeneration of soil, improving health and fertility of the landscape
Lower dams can hold grey water and act as aquaponics systems

### KEY POINT
The highest point on the property where water is naturally captured and stored. Located in valleys of secondary streams at the highest possible point of a hill's profile, where the slope profile changes from convex to concave.

Freely Available
www.permaculturedesign.ca

# DESIGN FOR WATER
## TECHNIQUES

**DAMS**

**- Key Point Dam**
Catches water at the key points, between key lines.
Used to store irrigation water.

**- Ridge Point Dam**
Used for run off and pumped storage and have limited irrigation use
Used for energy generation
Built on sub plateaus of flattened ridges below Saddle dams
Also known as horseshoe dams because its horseshoe shaped

**- Saddle Dam**
Useful for wildlife to drink from
Storage of water high in the landscape
Used for pumped water and energy generation
Has the highest available storage capacity
Resides on saddles or hollows in skyline profiles of hills circular or oblong shaped

**- Contour Dam**
Mainly used for irrigation, aquaculture and semi arid flood flow basins
Walls are built on contour, on slopes less than 8%

**- Check Dam**
Small, often temporary dam across swale, drainage ditch or waterway
Used to regulate and direct stream flow
Not used for water storage
May have a base pipe or fixed opening to allow for more manageable water flow
May have a base opening to keep the dam free of siltation

**- Barrier Dam**
Used for irrigation above main valleys
Used for energy systems
Constructed across flowing or intermittent stream beds
Need ample spillways, fish ladders and careful construction

**- Gabion Dam**
Used to create flat areas where silt loads can be usefully deposited and form absorption beds in flood conditions

**- Turkey Nest Dam**
Flat circular dam on level ground
Useful for stock water tanks and low head irrigation
Most commonly used in flatlands

Freely Available
www.permaculturedesign.ca

# DESIGN FOR WATER
## FACTS

**DEW**
- Is the droplets of water found on thin, exposed objects in the morning or evening
- In low temperature conditions dew becomes ice and is called frost
- Forms on on clear nights when moist air masses deposit water on the ground
- The dew point is the temperature at which air is cooled enough to condense water, it is a calculation of relative humidity and temperature
- Provides significant moisture availability to plants
- The best collectors are isolated from the ground which conducts heat so they are lower temperature than the ground
- Can be captured with piles of stones or shrubs
- Use metal wire fence with plantings along the drip line
- Dew ponds or 'cloud ponds' were used since medieval times in England, located on hilltops and lined with chalk, lime or clay, incorporating lime or soot prevents earthworms from coming up and making holes, they were often covered in straw to prevent cracking from sunlight, then layered with rubble and broken stone to protect the lining from the hooves of sheep or cattle drinking from it
- In modern India dew harvesting systems are used that can harvest up to 200 litres of water a night

**Source Curriculum:** Bill Mollison, David Holmgren, Rosemary Morrow, Toby Hemenway, Robin Clayfield, Larry Santoyo, Michael Becker, Looby Macnamara, Scott Pittman, Geoff Lawton, Robyn Francis, Mark Lakeman, Patricia Michael, Starhawk, Bullock Brothers, Tom Ward, Jude Hobbs, Doug Bullock, Brad Lancaster

**Envoy:** Delvin Solkinson www.visionarypermaculture.com

**Foundational Work :** Kym Chi www.gigglingchitree.com

**Gaiacraft Workbook Editing Team :** Delvin Solkinson, Kym Chi, Annaliese Hordern, Tamara Griffiths, Jacob Aman, Tes Tesla, Niki Hammond

**Design :** Sijay James www.onbeyondmetamedia.com

Freely Available
www.permaculturedesign.ca

# DESIGN FOR CLIMATE
## ENERGY CYCLES

**DESIGN FOR WATER**
- Soil and plants hold and transpire water, causing and regulating rainfall
- Water bodies regulate temperature by moderating the peaks of hot and cold on a daily and seasonal basis
- Distillation is water rising from the ground as a vapour
- Transpiration is water evaporating from plants during the daytime
- Guttation is water lost from the leaves as droplets during the night
- Dew is caused by moist air condensing on exposed surfaces
- Frost forms by rapidly cooling moist air bodies over land on cold, cloudless, still nights
- Fog comes from oceans and mountains, mostly in autumn and winter
- Fog forms where warm water evaporates into cool air, or where the cold earth condenses moisture from warmer air
- Water changing from ice to liquid to gas (evaporation) is accompanied by cooling
- Water changing from gas to liquid to ice (condensation) is accompanied by warming
- Rain is caused by
Orographic effects : cooling of air as it rises over mountains and hills
Cyclonic or frontal effects : over-riding of cool and warm air masses
Convectional effects : hot air rising from deserts or oceans into cooler air
- Humidity in air adds mass and reduces temperature changes (slows down temperature fluctuations and moderates overall temperature)

**FUNCTIONS OF PRECIPITATION**
- Bring water
- Hydrate
- Universal solvent
- Carry nutrients
- Move heat around
- Reduce temperature
- Cleanse air
- Transport (seeds, animals, minerals, bacteria)
- Indicate cycles of life and seasons
- Shape the land
- Stabilize soil
- Provide energy
- Put out fires

Freely Available
www.permaculturedesign.ca

# DESIGN FOR CLIMATE
## ENERGY CYCLES

### WIND
- Cool air is heavy and moves downhill
- Cool air flowing downhill that hits a barrier causes a 'cold sink'
- Cool air replaces hot air by going under it and pushing it up
- Hot air is light and moves uphill
- Hot air flowing uphill that hits a barrier causes a 'heat sink'
- Cold air flows off polar icecaps spinning low pressure systems counter clockwise in the northern hemisphere and clockwise in the southern hemisphere moving towards the equator from east to west
- Western coasts get alternating cold low pressure polar air systems with warm high pressure systems
- Deserts radiate heat upwards which sucks in cooler ocean air and causes monsoon climates

### FUNCTIONS OF WIND
- Transport (heat, cold, soil, sound, smells, pheromones)
- Shape the land
- Prune
- Pollenate
- Move clouds
- Evaporate water
- Provide energy
- Feed and drive fires
- Carry animals, birds and insects
- Oxygenate

*"Sitting at our back doorsteps, all we need to live a good life lies about us. Sun, wind, people, buildings, stones, sea, birds and plants surround us. Cooperation with all these things brings harmony, opposition to them brings disaster and chaos."*
- **Bill Mollison** www.tagari.com

Freely Available
www.permaculturedesign.ca

**PERMACULTURE WORKSHEET** 081

# DESIGN FOR CLIMATE
## ENERGY CYCLES

### LIGHT and HEAT
- Air and water can transfer heat to and from solid bodies (convection)
- Heat can be transferred between solid bodies touching (conduction)
- Light is radiated back as heat from soil and water, dark surfaces and when passed through glass
- Light colored objects reflect light
- Dense objects take longer to heat up but radiate heat longer
- Light absorbed by plants for photosynthesis has a cooling effect
- White light is turned to chemical energy by plants
- Dark green and red plants absorb more light and thus cool the environment
- Light coloured leaves and bark reflect light to increase ambient light in the forest
- Plants are a sink for carbon dioxide
- When forests are removed it can cause thermal pollution of too much light and heat
- Too much light will cause plants to dwarf
- Too little light will cause plants to become tall and straggly

### FUNCTIONS OF LIGHT
- Heat earth
- Melt snow
- Provide energy
- Evaporate water
- Cause wind and drive the hydrologic cycle
- Sterilize
- Stimulate chemical reactions
- Accelerate decomposition
- Make vitamin D
- Germinate

*"Life likes to park itself in gradients where there is flow
then apply patterns to catch and store energy without disturbing the flow."*
- **Toby Hemenway** www.tobyhemenway.com

Freely Available
www.permaculturedesign.ca

# DESIGN FOR CLIMATE
## MICROCLIMATES

### MICROCLIMATES
- Affects warming, cooling, and shading
- Crucial for placing plants, animals systems and structures
- Note the potential for creating or removing heat and cool sinks
- Some plants prefer morning or afternoon sun
- Design home and gardens to include resiliency against extreme weather conditions, buffering future climate variations
- To find the optimal angle of glazing on a greenhouse, take your latitude and add 15 degrees

### SLOPE
- Aspect comes from the degree the site is facing the sun and affects exposure to sun and hours of sunlight
- The steeper the slope the faster hot air moves up it and the faster water moves down it
- The steeper the slope the faster fire travels up hill
- The higher the altitude, the lower the temperature
- Any slope more than 15 degrees should be treed

### SOIL AND ROCKS
- Affect absorption and evaporation of water into the environment
- Rocks capture and slowly radiate heat
- Clay soil holds more water, expands and contracts
- Sandy soil drains well and does not hold water long
- Bare, lighter colored soils reflect light while darker and mulched soils absorb light and radiate heat
- Dark soil that is not dense will heat up fastest

### WATER
- Humidifies air
- Cools warm air and warms cool air
- Has a more stable temperature and makes the temperature of surrounding areas more moderate
- Provides water for beneficial animals and insects
- Maritime climates give cool late day winds to relieve land of daytime heat

Freely Available
www.permaculturedesign.ca

# DESIGN FOR CLIMATE
## MICROCLIMATES

**STRUCTURES**
- Trap and store energy
- Create thermal mass
- Reflect light
- Act as a windbreak
- Buffer noise
- Add vertical areas for growing intensively
- Create social microclimates

**VEGETATION**
- Absorbs heat and light
- Regulates soil temperature (warmer in winter, cooler in summer)
- Transpiration of plants will cool air in summer
- Provides habitat, windbreaks, shelterbelts, and firebelts which filter and capture nutrients, weed seed and disease from wind
- Windbreaks are effective to about 5 times their height in distance on the other side and require 40% flow through of air for success
- Germination of plants and ripening of fruits is affected by light and heat
- Biotecture is the use of living plants in the design of structures and can be used to create microclimates

**KEY STRATEGIES**
- Modify extremes
- Catch and store energy (water, wind and light)
- Convert light into heat
- Convert light into life
- Reflect light to be absorbed by areas needing more light or heat
- Block strong climatological effects
- Protect gardens, plants and structures
- Create microclimates to increase diversity
- Site houses or gardens on heat sinks or thermal belts of higher average temperature
- Choose and place appropriate animals, structures and farm elements for your climate
- Light and temperature increases as one moves from the pole to the equator

Freely Available
www.permaculturedesign.ca

# DESIGN FOR CLIMATE
## WORLD CLIMATE

**WORLD CLIMATE CHARACTERISTICS**
- characterized by temperature and rainfall
- Tropical : no month under 18 degrees
- Subtropical : coolest months above 0 degrees
- Temperate : cold months below 0 degrees and warmest month above 10 degrees
- Polar : warmest month below 10 degrees
- Arid : annual rainfall lower than 50 cm
- Desert : annual rainfall below 25 cm
- Maritime climates are more moderate and Continental climates are more extreme
- Humid landscapes are shaped by water and have rolling forms
- Cool landscapes are shaped by ice and have tall, steep slopes
- Dry landscapes are shaped by wind and have vertical slopes and gullies

**CLIMATE CHANGE**
Globally, we are still grappling with the reality that our climate is changing and that the cause of this is complex. Glaciers and regions of permafrost are melting due to increased temperatures, which has resulted in climatic changes and unpredictable weather patterns. These changes have encouraged us to become more resourceful in our planning for the coming times.

"The world I would like to see is a world in which my grandchildren can thrive, where they will live in local economies, feel like part of a place, and be more skilled. I would like them to live in a world where they view the climate crisis in the way we now think about the ozone crisis, as something in the past that people came together to address and is steadily becoming less and less of a threat and challenge. I would like them to see the world around flourishing and coming alive. One where the ingenuity, creativity and adaptability that created the industrial revolution in the first place becomes what defines their life as we move away from fossil fuels into something so much more beautiful, abundant and nourishing."
- Rob Hopkins www.transitionnetwork.org

**Source Curriculum:** Bill Mollison, David Holmgren, Rosemary Morrow, Toby Hemenway, Robin Clayfield, Larry Santoyo, Michael Becker, Looby Macnamara, Scott Pittman, Geoff Lawton, Robyn Francis, Mark Lakeman, Patricia Michael, Starhawk, Bullock Brothers, Tom Ward, Jude Hobbs

**Envoy:** Delvin Solkinson www.visionarypermaculture.com

**Foundational Work :** Kym Chi www.gigglingchitree.com

**Gaiacraft Workbook Editing Team :** Delvin Solkinson, Kym Chi, Annaliese Hordern, Tamara Griffiths, Jacob Aman, Tes Tesla, Niki Hammond

**Design :** Sijay James www.onbeyondmetamedia.com

Freely Available
www.permaculturedesign.ca

# DESIGN FOR CLIMATE
## APPROPRIATE TECHNOLOGY

### COOKING
- Cook shared meals
- Choose renewable resources for fuel
- Obtain multiple functions from a heat source
- Eat canned and dried food in the winter
- Eat local
- Eat raw food
- Build a solar oven to bring food to boiling temperature then place into a hay or otherwise insulated box to continue cooking
- Grow coppicing plants to harvest and store for fire wood and know where to collect smaller kindling sticks
- Rocket stoves use smaller sticks to create a high heat. Smaller sticks burn at a higher temperature, are more efficient, are more easily obtained over time from a coppice system. They are a better use of resources than larger logs.

### HEATING, COOLING AND LIGHTING STRUCTURES
- Practice seasonal living
- Wear a sweater and layer clothes
- Share body heat
- Follow daytime and night time light patterns
- Use candles
- Passive heating and cooling
- Insulate house
- Seal windows and repair gaps where cold air creeps in
- Use heavy curtains and pelmets or cornice boards to insulate windows
- Paint interiors with light and reflective surfaces
- Methane generation by compost from plant matter or manure
- Generate electricity from heat (from woodstove)

### WATER HEATING
- Passive and solar thermal hot water heating
- Wash clothes in cold water and by hand
- Use hot water sparingly
- Keep tap turned off when not in use
- Use a washbasin for washing dishes, collect dish water and reuse
- Heat water on woodstove or rocket mass heater
- Insulate water tank and pipes
- Use a thermos to store excess boiling water after making a cup of tea

Freely Available
www.permaculturedesign.ca

**PERMACULTURE WORKSHEET 086**

# DESIGN FOR CLIMATE
## APPROPRIATE TECHNOLOGY

**APPLIANCES**
- Downsize systems
- Use hand and pedal powered technologies
- Eliminate the need for electric cold storage by using local and fresh food
- Use passive cooling and refrigeration techniques
- Use high efficiency, low tech electrical appliances
- Disconnect appliances that use phantom power
- Bicycle generator
- Research before buying

**TRANSPORTATION**
- Relocalize
- Live and work in the same area
- Walk more often
- Prioritize biking & trailers
- Use public transport
- Car share and carpool
- Prioritize train over plane
- Biological energy (biofuel, alcohol, sugar)

**WORK AND RIGHT LIVELIHOOD**
- Do work that you love
- Do work to satisfy real needs
- Support socially just practices
- Purchase local goods and services
- Work as a means to support community networks
- Participate in alternative forms of trading your time and skills
- Eliminate waste
- Work in co-operative settings
- Support regenerative systems
- Use your body and get outside
- Create a healthy work environment

Freely Available
www.permaculturedesign.ca

**PERMACULTURE WORKSHEET 087**

# DESIGN FOR CLIMATE
## APPROPRIATE TECHNOLOGY

**FOOD**
- Think and act regionally
- Support local growers and food systems
- Join a CSA (Community Supported Agriculture)
- Join your local seed savers
- Start a community seed bank
- Shop at co-ops
- Eat a low carbon diet (more veg, less meat)
- Grow your own garden
- Raise your own animals
- Develop community gardens and orchards
- Salvage from the waste stream
- Support and develop progressive food policies
- Support or create local 'Food is Free' or 'Food not Bombs' initiatives

*"My hopes for permaculture range from the most general to the most specific. As a concept I hope it continues to be informed and infused with creative thinking and activism that arises from outside its own self referenced world. In this way it will avoid stagnation in thinking and action and continue to exhibit hybrid vigour that can respond to a rapidly changing world. This inclusive mentality that acknowledges like minded concepts and networks reduces the problems of "turf warfare" between pioneering concepts that colonise the psycho social margins of mainstream society.*

*This holistic "jack of all trades" scope of permaculture needs to be balanced by a "mastery of one". For each of us that calling and contribution to a better world will be many and varied. My hope is that enough permaculture practitioners dedicated their lives to making the founding permaculture vision of truly productive bioregional tree crop agricultures a reality able to survive the rigours of climate change and energy descent."*
- David Holmgren www.holmgren.com.au

**Source Curriculum:** Mark Lakeman www.cityrepair.org, Doug Bullock www permacultureportal.com

**Envoy:** Delvin Solkinson www.visionarypermaculture.com

**Foundational Work :** Kym Chi www.gigglingchitree.com

**Gaiacraft Workbook Editing Team :** Delvin Solkinson, Kym Chi, Annaliese Hordern, Tamara Griffiths, Jacob Aman, Tes Tesla, Niki Hammond

**Design :** Sijay James www.onbeyondmetamedia.com

Freely Available
**www.permaculturedesign.ca**

**PERMACULTURE WORKSHEET 088**

# DESIGN FOR CLIMATE
## CLIMATE ANALOGUES

**SUNSHINE COAST AND GREATER VANCOUVER BIOREGION**
49.4° N Latitude, 123.6° W Longitude
Lower Sunshine Coast
On the Pacific Ocean protected by Vancouver Island
Sea level to 100 metres above sea level
Days of Rain 167
Yearly Rain Average 1369 mm
Days of Snow 10
Yearly Snow Average 236 cm
Temperature Range -15 to +30
First frost : Beginning of November
Last frost : End of March
Relatively mild winters with little snow
Cold air from the Arctic that sweeps over the rest of Canada in winter is blocked by the Rocky Mountains
Moderating Maritime influence of the Pacific
Wet and Foggy
Average of 10 Days of snowfall at sea level
Wet Winters and Sunny Summers
Well defined Spring and Autumn
Not too windy
- USDA plant hardiness
Average minimum temperature
We are 8a to 9a in the milder zones
- Koppen-Geiger
Temperature and precipitation + their seasonality
West coast maritime. We are Cfb to Csb in the dryer zones
- Analogue Locations
Christchurch, New Zealand
Stanley, Tasmania
Concepcion, Chile
Sendai, Japan
Ordu, Turkey
Canterbury, England
Cardiff, Wales
Paris, France
Antwerp, Belgium
Amsterdam, Netherlands
Frankfurt, Germany

Freely Available
www.permaculturedesign.ca

**PERMACULTURE WORKSHEET 089**

# DESIGN FOR CLIMATE
## CLIMATE ANALOGUES

Cool climate plants of interest at **Bullocks Permaculture Homestead**
Azola - Salviniaceae
Hardy Kiwi - Actinidia arguta
Fuzzy Kiwi - Actinidia deliciosa
Monkey Puzzle - Araucaria araucana
Chokeberry - Aronia melancarpa
Darwin Barberry - Berberis darwinii
America Chestnut - Castanea dentata
Chinese Chestnut - Castanea mollissima
Sweet Chestnut - Castanea sativa
Ceanothus Victoria - Ceanothus thyrsiflorus
Bladder Senna - Colutea aborescens
Cornelian or Capulin Cherry - Cornus mas
Common Quince - Cydonia bologna
Russian olive - Elaeagnus angustifolia
Goumi - Elaeagnus multiflora
Autumn olive - Elaeagnus umbellata
Desert King Fig - Ficus Desert King
French Broom - Genista monospessulana
Chilean Hazel - Gevunia avellana
Honeylocust - Gleditsia triacanthos
Sea-buckthorns - Hippophae rhamnoides
Heartnut - Juglans ailantifolia
English Walnut - Juglans regia
Chilean Myrtle - Luma apiculate
Medlar - Mespilus germanica
White Mulberry - Morus alba
Everbearing Mulberry - Morus rubra x nigra
Mulberry - Morus nigra
Empress Tree - Paulownia tomentosa
Italian Stone Pine - Pinus pinna
Korean Stone Pine - Pinus koraiensis
Fan Palm - Trachycarpus
American Plum - Prunus armeniaca
Black Locust - Robina pseudoacacia
Shipova - X Sorbopyrus auricularis
Persimmons - Persimmon
Hardy Citrus - Yuzu Ichandrin
Wild Yam - Yamaimo discorea Japonica

Freely Available
www.permaculturedesign.ca

**PERMACULTURE WORKSHEET 090**

# DESIGN FOR CLIMATE
## CLIMATE ANALOGUES

Find places with similar climates to your own by following lines of latitude in order to learn what might work in your area

Climate Analogues can teach us about what plants and animals from elsewhere in the world may thrive. Also what techniques and strategies may help us design for climate and microclimate. This includes elements related to energy and water, structures and fencing, composting and soil, pests and predators, forestry and farming.

**LOCATING ANALOGUES BASED ON**
- Levels of latitude on both sides of the equator
- Highs and lows
- Seasonal variation
- Latitude on both sides of equator
- Distance from Ocean or large bodies of water
- Elevation
- Temperature
- Precipitation
- Wind
- Plant hardiness zones

**Source Curriculum:** Sam and Doug Bullock www.permacultureportal.com
**Envoy:** Delvin Solkinson www.visionarypermaculture.com
**Foundational Work :** Kym Chi www.gigglingchitree.com
**Gaiacraft Workbook Editing Team :** Delvin Solkinson, Kym Chi, Annaliese Hordern, Tamara Griffiths, Jacob Aman, Tes Tesla, Niki Hammond
**Design :** Sijay James www.onbeyondmetamedia.com

Freely Available
www.permaculturedesign.ca

**PERMACULTURE WORKSHEET 091**

# DESIGN FOR COOL CLIMATE
## SEASONAL LIFE

As part of becoming conscious global citizens, we are learning about the world's climates and how we can design intentionally to account for climatic factors.

### CHARACTERISTICS
- Precipitation exceeds evaporation
- There are below freezing temperatures
- Mild to warm summers and cold winters
- Most nutrient is stored in the soil which has high humus content and holds a lot of water
- Streams are often acidic with tannins, saponins and humic acids

### CHALLENGES
- Industrialization and cars create acid rain which degrades soil and water quality
- Pesticides and industrial toxins
- Loss of top soil through conventional agriculture and deforestation
- Compaction from precipitation, industrial farming and animals husbandry
- Exposure to fog, frost, snow, ice, hail and cold wind
- Most plant growth occurs in spring and summer only
- High cost of space and water heating
- Slugs, pests and wild animals
- Forest fires

### STRATEGIES
- Make sure cold air can flow downhill
- Keyline damming and swale systems for gravity fed irrigation and water management
- Radiation shields of white rock, trees or hedgerows facing the fire sector
- Animals with good structures near home
- Use of plant and animal guilds to address pest issues and feed the soil
- Lime soils to balance acidity
- Feed soils
- Windbreaks and permanent forest edges to protect from wind and fire
- Native plants for windbreaks and mulch
- Include short season plant varieties
- Seasonal flooding

Freely Available
www.permaculturedesign.ca

# DESIGN FOR COOL CLIMATE
## SEASONAL LIFE

- Site houses on a midslope key point (on thermal belt)
- Good aspect exposure for winter sun
- Site house downhill from forest and water storage
- Good insulation of houses, pipes, and wells
- Locate pipes and build foundations for structures and fences below the frost line
- Thermal mass foundations
- Insulate beneath foundations with frost wings
- Good drainage below and around house
- Sloped roof for rain and snow runoff
- Sheltered with walls, earthbanks or hedgerows on upslope side
- Suntrap fedges on the upslope shade side
- Trellis vines on sunside
- Deciduous trees on afternoon sun side
- Double entries to houses, barns, and greenhouses
- Seal windows, doors and gaps
- In-house food preservation and storage facilities
- Wood stove or rocket stove for heating, cooking, baking, dehydrating, drying
- Bedrooms on cool side of the house
- Living areas on the sun side of the house
- Attic ventilation
- Greenhouse attached to main house for heat
- Attach greenhouse to sunside and shadehouse to shade side
- Fan that can spin counter-clockwise to push cool air downward, or spin clockwise to pull cold air up
- Extend growing season and modify extremes with greenhouses, glasshouses, hoop houses, cold frames, hot frame, walipinis
- Passive solar greenhouse : one sided, angled roof facing sun, thermal mass light colored wall on shade side, deciduous trellis over roof, vented, could be converted into shade house
- Composts in greenhouse
- Thermal mass
- Small windows on morning sun side
- Few windows on afternoon sun side
- Window curtains
- Eaves and windows designed to let in afternoon winter sun, but not afternoon summer sun

Freely Available
www.permaculturedesign.ca

**PERMACULTURE WORKSHEET 093**

# DESIGN FOR COOL CLIMATE
## SEASONAL LIFE

- Setting the Roof Overhang
Winter Solstice sun angle "A": A = 90° − (your latitude + 23.5°)
Summer Solstice sun angle "A": A = 90° − (Your latitude − 23.5°)
Knowing this, you can use trigonometry to set your roof overhang so that you let sun in during the winter and keep it out during the summer.

**GARDEN AND FARM**
- Mixed forests, hedgerows, orchards
- Food forests and farm forestry
- Fruit, nut and syrup trees
- Perennial berry crops
- Mushroom cultivation
- Perennial pastures and grasslands for people and animals
- Meadows, small fields and veggie plots
- Herb spirals and keyhole beds
- Alley cropping
- Pasture cropping
- Integration of fedge sun traps
- Fresh water aquaculture
- Animals : bees, chickens, turkeys, ducks, geese, pheasant, quail, guinea hens, snakes, frogs, fish like trout and sturgeon, rabbits, pigs, goats, sheep, cows, horses, emu, ostrich, kangaroo, llama, bison, deer
- Rocks, stick piles and stone walls
- Covered winter garden
- Cool hardy and frost tolerant species
- Planting nitrogen fixers, bioaccumulators, spike root plants and biodynamics herbs
- Grow root crops for winter storage
- No-till gardening
- Heavy mulching of gardens

**Source Curriculum:** Bill Mollison, David Holmgren, Rosemary Morrow, Toby Hemenway, Robin Clayfield, Larry Santoyo, Michael Becker, Looby Macnamara, Scott Pittman, Geoff Lawton, Robyn Francis, Mark Lakeman, Patricia Michael, Starhawk, Bullock Brothers, Tom Ward, Jude Hobbs

**Envoy:** Delvin Solkinson www.visionarypermaculture.com

**Foundational Work :** Kym Chi www.gigglingchitree.com

**Gaiacraft Workbook Editing Team :** Delvin Solkinson, Kym Chi, Annaliese Hordern, Tamara Griffiths, Jacob Aman, Tes Tesla, Niki Hammond

**Design :** Sijay James www.onbeyondmetamedia.com

Freely Available
www.permaculturedesign.ca

**PERMACULTURE WORKSHEET 094**

# DESIGN FOR TROPICS
## ABUNDANT LIFE

### CHARACTERISTICS
- Rampant growth and decomposition
- Most nutrient stored in trees and plants
- Soils tend to be acidic due to excessive rains leaching out nutrients

### SUBCLIMATES

Wet Tropics
- River basins and wet coasts, overhead sun, temperature
- Temperature 21 - 32 degrees C
- Rainfall from 152 - 328 cm

Wet-Dry Tropics
- Towards the poles of wet tropics, dry hot winters
- Low humidity
- Temperature 21 - 38 degrees C, rainfall from 25 - 162 cm

Monsoon Tropics
- Cooler winters and wet summers and autumns
- Temperature 13 - 38 degrees C
- Rainfall 102 - 1016 cm

### CHALLENGES
- Erosion from heavy rain fall
- Pests and disease
- Polluted water
- Nutrient poor soils
- Flooding
- Sea level rise
- Strong winds
- Unstable climate conditions with surprises
- Annual veggies are battered by the force of tropical rain and invaded by fungi and pest
- Wet and Wet-dry Tropics: heat and high rainfall leach most mobile nutrients from soils, vegetation and animals contain 80 - 90% of nutrients, rapid runoff and evaporation
- Dry Tropics: heat
- Monsoon Tropics: tsunamis, hurricanes and intense weather systems

Freely Available
www.permaculturedesign.ca

# DESIGN FOR TROPICS
## ABUNDANT LIFE

**STRATEGIES**
- Preserve trees
- River vs road transport
- Valley sites for shading
- Site sheltered from climate extremes and disasters
- Water storage
- Design for drainage
- Plan for large seasonal rain periods
- Particular attention to grey water and black water processing
- Terracing on slopes to hold water in landscape and for seasonal crop rotations between water crops and dry crops
- Erosion control with grass and tree plantings
- Extensive use of grass crops and forage legumes to chop and drop
- Living mulches for wet season, dry mulches for dry season
- Integrated pest management
- No use of plastic or metal (due to leaching and rapid breakdown)
- Smoke cooking inside, is taking care of mosquitos and curing the thatch roof (raise roof instead of changing tech)

*"My passion for permaculture comes from the living earth, my family and friends, present and past. I feel the need to build a better, peaceful and productive world. Every day I am inspired by permaculture. We spend far too much time being 'human doings' and not enough as 'human beings'. Once you 'get' Permaculture, it becomes who you are, an unconscious blend in your life of trying to find means to work less and waste less, to share knowledge and understanding, produce with others, make better buildings and harvest the energy we use as much as possible. If all else fails I go in the garden. In 1990 we realized that Permaculture is 'Revolution disguised as organic gardening'. Gardening is a magnificent gateway into understanding how the principles of Permaculture work in a manageable achievable and rewarding way. To paraphrase William Congreve 'Gardening hath charms to soothe a savage breast'. I don't see my life's work and leisure as distinguished. Everything I do has a purpose and should also bring pleasure to me and others. To me all living things are people and kindness sits at the heart of the human future."*
- **Graham Bell** www.grahambell.org

Freely Available
www.permaculturedesign.ca

**PERMACULTURE WORKSHEET 096**

# DESIGN FOR TROPICS
## ABUNDANT LIFE

**GARDEN AND FARM**
- Careful planting and harvesting schedule to match climate
- High diversity of species and harvests
- Consideration of pests
- No standing water
- Interplanted stacked food forest (mixed multi-story polycultural system including plants for mulch and soil building)
- Mounded beds for drainage
- Raised beds
- No-dig gardening
- Never plough because of rains and dry seasons
- Use of green crops, living mulches and nitrogen fixers
- Rough and heavy mulching with woody materials (wood, like all organic materials, breaks down rapidly in the tropics)
- Passive on-demand hot water
- Aquaculture systems
- Focus on herbaceous perennials
- Tubers, vines, shrubs, trees for food
- Integrated hedgerows
- Forests for timber, oil, sugar and thatch
- Pit composting
- Takakura compost : indoor system using rice/corn husks (carbon) and microorganism
- Banana circles
- Composting super plants include azola, limbna and palms
- Use of ants and termites
- Weed barriers
- No bare soil
- Covered nursery areas to protect seedlings from high rainfall
- Chinampas: islands or peninsulas created by dredging high nutrient material from the bottom of pond, swamp or lake to grow water loving crops in wet environments. Often accessed by boat or narrow trail
- Stacking in time with succession to protect soils
- Terraces
- For gardening with annuals clear small area, garden or farm, then move location
- Wet Tropics : grey and black water systems, intensive cultivation
- Wet-dry Tropics: shelterbelts, firebreaks, reclaiming eroded lands with pioneer plants, soakage pits, key line damming, manure fertilization
- Monsoon Tropics : design for disaster, heavy tree cover and windbreaks, tsunamis, hurricanes and intense weather systems

  Freely Available
www.permaculturedesign.ca

**PERMACULTURE WORKSHEET 097**

# DESIGN FOR TROPICS
## ABUNDANT LIFE

### HOUSE AND STRUCTURES
- Orientation to prevailing winds (not sun)
- Site home in valleys
- Site houses away from areas where mudslides are an issue (typically from tree removal)
- Low energy-use houses
- Over-shading trees, trellises and thatched (palm / grasses) roofs or metal roofs
- White walls and roof
- Houses use natural local timbers or fibres, sometimes clays
- Often have no walls
- Plantings inside and on outside walls
- Shaded open-air kitchen separate from house
- Passive ventilation and louvers
- Underground pipes with cool air from shaded cool sink
- Attached shadehouse to shade-side of house and attached greenhouse to sun-side of house
- Shade house brings in cool air, sunhouse utilizes hot air and together they create a ventilation system
- Well insulated and passive ventilation
- May be raised off the ground
- Above tsunami height
- Wide verandas and eves with shade trellises
- Insect screens
- Cellar/underground shelter
- Houses use natural material, often have no walls
- Building off the ground
- Could include floating houses or tree houses
- Often use bamboo and feather palm
- Covered outdoor work, walk ways and storage spaces

**Source Curriculum:** Bill Mollison, David Holmgren, Rosemary Morrow, Toby Hemenway, Robin Clayfield, Larry Santoyo, Michael Becker, Looby Macnamara, Scott Pittman, Geoff Lawton, Robyn Francis, Mark Lakeman, Patricia Michael, Starhawk, Bullock Brothers, Tom Ward, Jude Hobbs

**Envoy:** Delvin Solkinson www.visionarypermaculture.com

**Foundational Work :** Kym Chi www.gigglingchitree.com

**Gaiacraft Workbook Editing Team :** Delvin Solkinson, Kym Chi, Annaliese Hordern, Tamara Griffiths, Jacob Aman, Tes Tesla, Niki Hammond

**Design :** Sijay James www.onbeyondmetamedia.com

Freely Available
www.permaculturedesign.ca

**PERMACULTURE WORKSHEET 098**

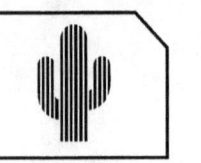

# DESIGN FOR DRYLANDS
## PLANT LIFE

**CHARACTERISTICS**
- Evaporation exceeds condensation
- Desert is rich with high nutrient biomass in suspension
- Hot summers with mild to cold winters

**CHALLENGES**
- Aridity
- Salinization
- Episodic rain with periods of drought
- Winds
- Poisons lingering in the soil
- Wild animals and pests
- Episodic flooding with periods of drought
- Extreme heat
- Erosion
- Often sandy or alkaline soils
- Loss of topsoil
- Desertification

*"The best way to become a permaculture actionary is to do two things at once: Stare our epoch in the face and see as many of it's imperfections as you can, feel them. Then, in the same moment, realize that the other side of each challenge is another design opportunity that is available to you to grasp and express through action. Yes, human cultures have designed all of our own problems, and the flip side of each one is a missed design opportunity. We are here in this time to inhabit these conditions and to activate in response to them. I did these two things at once, and at that same moment someone said to me that "the very creative impulse of our planet is under attack, and through our choices it will or will not endure". That was just too damn much, and I haven't stopped being relentless in my active advocacy and love for our planet home ever since."*
- **Mark Lakeman** www.cityrepair.org

Freely Available
www.permaculturedesign.ca

**PERMACULTURE WORKSHEET 099**

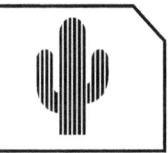

# DESIGN FOR DRYLANDS
## PLANT LIFE

**STRATEGIES**
- Everything you do must reduce evaporation and increase condensation
- Planting trees
- Protect existing Biocrust and create more where ethically possible
- Protecting existing vegetation
- Design for water catchment, storage and retention
- Capture moisture from air and harvest dew
- Water and soil testing
- Wild crafting and hunting instead of herding
- Utilize exotic rivers, oases and aquifers ethically
- Store water for cooking and drinking
- Increase water input to aquifer and rehumidify desert air with vegetation
- Use wastewater in gardens
- Minimal watering of garden and farm
- Shredded bark, manure and leaf nutrient mulches
- Gravel mulch reduces erosion while catching windburn soil and seeds
- Utilize succession starting with native, drought resistant pioneer species
- No use of biocides, pesticides or fertilizers
- Utilize rain catchment and shade patterns from landscape features with contours and slope
- Prevent erosion with contour banks and tree cover
- Gather rain runoff with shaded swales, treelines, deep ripped contours, gabions, limonia, silt dams, and lines of stones
- Focus on soil building and soil feeding
- Have back up systems and a diversity of techniques
- Key focus on establishment techniques
- Shape land to hold organic matter, soil and water
- Small scale animals systems with rotational grazing
- Look at how many animals the land can sustain and how long it can sustain them for
- Recycle and reuse water while regulating use

Freely Available
www.permaculturedesign.ca

**PERMACULTURE WORKSHEET 100**

# DESIGN FOR DRYLANDS
## PLANT LIFE

**HOME AND STRUCTURES**
- Site houses for shade and prevailing winds and close to water
- Need for summer/day cooling and winter/night heating means incorporating techniques found in both tropical and temperate housing
- Earthships and biotecture
- Interchangeable white and black colors on walls and rooves
- Shaded interior open-air courtyards and breezeways with seating areas
- Afternoon sun wall, windowless and shaded by evergreens
- Morning sun and full sun walls partially shaded with trees and shadehouses
- Small windows with blinds, slatted or latticed for shade and wind protection while retaining view
- Full sun-facing areas with windows that can be covered and insulated
- Summer/day outdoor kitchen and winter/night indoor kitchen
- Trellised vines on all walls, roofs, arbors and shade structures as solar and dust screens
- Underground storage and living spaces
- Ventilation
- Dry composting toilets
- Low pressure showers
- Roof water collection and shade side water storage
- Underground water tanks and cisterns
- Good insulation to keep cool or heat in depending upon season and time of day
- Earth tunnels from below the house to draw in cool air
- Solar panels and windmills
- Shade side shadehouse and sun side sunhouse
- Greenhouse for winter heat, to catch and release solar heat, to dry food and protect it from pests
- Utilise evapotranspiration from plants in home
- Rammed earth buildings
- Weather proof and pest proof
- Underground, dug-outs, Earth bermed

Freely Available
www.permaculturedesign.ca

**PERMACULTURE WORKSHEET 101**

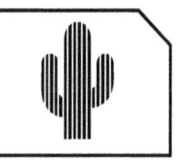

# DESIGN FOR DRYLANDS
## PLANT LIFE

**GARDEN AND FARM**
- Heavy mulching on surface and subsurface
- Shade by cloth, structures and trees
- Intensive small scale gardening
- Drip watered composting pits
- Depressed garden beds with raised edges
- Net and pan, staggered rows of trees on slope, pan shaped micro-berm on downslope with overflow diversion drain to other trees downslope
- Micro catchments around plantings
- Swales covered with rocks or soils and planted with hardy trees
- Rocks for shelter, microclimate niches, water runoff, condensation and rentention
- Windbreaks or fences
- Multitudes of small windbreaks of sand resistant heat hearty, drought tolerant plants
- Create soak barriers across landscape with stone cages or walls
- Protect young trees from strong winds using tree guards
- Shade cloths over garden beds
- Shade and protect seedlings from sun, wind and water erosion
- Utilize vertical spaces with trellises
- Design dryland planting guilds
- Encourage succession of plantings towards climax communities
- Ants and termites aerate soil and compost organic matter
- Use of tubers, bulbs, herbs, shrubs and deep rooting perennials
- Drought tolerant species of plants and animals
- Wild foods and traditional staple foods
- Interplanting with humus, mulch plants and ground covers
- Animals: guinea pigs, donkeys, birds, lizards, antelope, kangaroo, wallaby, camel, quail, pigeon, duck, geese, insects
- Possible to include a small amount of: goats, cattle, sheep if kept in small area and food is brought to them instead of grazing.
- Brush, scrub or bramble living fences
- Sunken, lined, wicking beds
- Aquaponics
- Sulphur to reduce pH
- Foliar feeds
- Movable shade houses
- Plant pioneer trees first to create shade and windbreak
- Pitting and imprinting
- Regenerate biocrust
- Earth bags and rammed earth

  Freely Available
www.permaculturedesign.ca

**PERMACULTURE WORKSHEET 102**

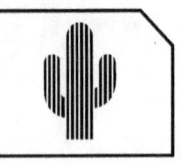

# DESIGN FOR DRYLANDS
## PLANT LIFE

Many plants that are grown as perennials in a temperate climate will grow as annuals in an arid environment, usually in the cooler months. Having a shady area for these plants to grow and plenty of water may keep them alive over the hotter months. For important plants, give them space in your zone one wicking bed. It may be necessary to dry your home-grown plants and use a powder in your compost, compost tea or in the garden. Dry matter may have a slightly different nutrient content.

Perennial arid land plants Lucerne and Old Man saltbush between them give us N, K, Ph, Mg, Ca, S, Mn, Mo, Cl, Na, Se.
Once Borage is established it is perennial and adds Ni.
Nettles grow as winter weeds in arid lands adding Fe and Cu.

### PRIMARY ELEMENTS

**N - NITROGEN**
Lucerne, Stinging nettle, Dandelion, Saltbush

**K - POTASSIUM**
Lucerne, Chamomile, Stinging nettle, Oak bark, Dandelion, Borage, Saltbush, Watercress, Purslane

**P - PHOSPHOROUS**
Lucerne, Chamomile, Dandelion, Lamb's quarters (fat hen), Saltbush

### SECONDARY ELEMENTS

**MG - MAGNESIUM**
Lucerne, Saltbush, Purslane, Stinging nettle, Sow Thistle, Watercress

**CA - CALCIUM**
Lucerne, Chamomile, Stinging Nettles, Fat Hen, Central Australian fig (Ficus platypode), Saltbush, Cleavers, Watercress

**S - SULPHUR**
Lucerne, Stinging Nettle, Garlic, Saltbush, Watercress

Freely Available
www.permaculturedesign.ca

# DESIGN FOR DRYLANDS
## PLANT LIFE

**MINOR ELEMENTS**

**FE - IRON**
Dandelion, Stinging nettle

**B - BORON**
Euphorbia spp.

**MN - MANGANESE**
Saltbush

**MO - MOLYBDENUM**
Lucerne, Saltbush, Walnuts, Almonds, Sunflower seeds, Lentils, Beans

**CL - CHLORINE**
Saltbush

**CU - COPPER**
Stinging Nettle, Dandelion, Legumes

**ZN - ZINC**
Legumes

**SI - SILICON**
Legumes, Borage

**NI - NICKEL**
Borage

**CO - COBALT**
Vetches

**Na - SODIUM**
Saltbush, Watercress

**Se - SELENIUM**
Saltbush

  Freely Available
www.permaculturedesign.ca

# DESIGN FOR DRYLANDS
## PLANT LIFE

*"We do not own the land, it owns us, and the land is sad for the loss of our careful attention and disturbances. The human heart longs for usefulness, engagement and biological entanglement. Permaculture moves us back toward home, to things we once all knew as people of place, and held in common stories and practices, all local and specific. Ooooh, my heart grows faint with the promise of relationship and reciprocation, in the place where my macro-molecules will one day be reassembled in some new emergent complexity. By helping whole systems thinking to stay sane while the big systems ride their adjustments and we tinker in some corner, Permaculture is a method of persistence. The crazy horizontal spread of permaculture education has sent out a lot of experimenters and public speakers to entertain change in the face of corporate consolidation. An academic origin gave permaculture just enough of a design based education template. For most every ecosystem inhabitation we can collect ecological knowledge, reassemble patterns and preserve precautionary principles. And away it goes. Where it ends no body knows. At least we know a good wave to jump on when it rolls by. Think about how the water stays in place while the wave passes through. All the local denizens are busy while some skimmers take a bigger look. Who else is taking the bigger look? Lots of indigenous councils and intact, but battered, traditions are there with us. The world does not need us to save it. The job is saving human culture and the memory and continuity of co-evolution and biodiversity building. Nancy Turner calls this "Keeping it Living". Metastasis. Many other academic institutions of ecological design have carried on with whole systems science and Permaculture just keeps teaching and implementing forward on the ground all over the planet. What Wendell Berry calls "Doing the right thing" means learning to live an engaged life on a low financial budget. We need to learn to live local and good, but poor. Re-skilling and Transition Towns are necessary, and so is what Scott Pittman calls "nurturing that design mind with good pedagogy". Permaculture offers the special gift of peoples' applied design process for kick-starting re-indigenation."*
- Tom Ward www.siskiyoupermaculture.com

**Source Curriculum:** Bill Mollison, David Holmgren, Rosemary Morrow, Toby Hemenway, Robin Clayfield, Larry Santoyo, Michael Becker, Looby Macnamara, Scott Pittman, Geoff Lawton, Robyn Francis, Mark Lakeman, Patricia Michael, Starhawk, Bullock Brothers, Tom Ward, Jude Hobbs

**Envoy:** Delvin Solkinson www.visionarypermaculture.com

**Foundational Work :** Kym Chi www.gigglingchitree.com

**Gaiacraft Workbook Editing Team :** Delvin Solkinson, Kym Chi, Annaliese Hordern, Tamara Griffiths, Jacob Aman, Tes Tesla, Niki Hammond

**Design :** Sijay James www.onbeyondmetamedia.com

Freely Available
www.permaculturedesign.ca

**PERMACULTURE WORKSHEET 105**

# DESIGN
## FINAL PROJECT

During your mapping process, write down the many design insights and ideas that come up. Once a foundational map has been established, ideally after a year of careful, documented observation, comes a permaculture design. The mapping continues alongside the design process, as both are ongoing processes that are always underway. The mainframe design approach starts with assessing and designing water systems, then access, then structures and finally plant and animal systems.

Use your base map as a foundation and add any elements you would like to see based on a needs assessment. Consider zones, sectors, microclimates, relative location, permaculture principles, ethics and techniques along with anything else covered in the permaculture design course.

Designing is an opportunity to review everything you have learned and think about how it applies to your own life and land. Flipping through the permaculture handouts and text books, as well as downloading the cards can bring you many ideas to evolve your design process.

Do a short writeup about the design including information about the reason and function for everything you are doing. In this writeup see how many references you can make to permaculture material. Doing an Integral Design means everything can be described from the perspective of functionality, closing energy loops while creating something efficient, effective and ethical.

For example perhaps we could connect a greenhouse to the south side of a main house and inside include a kitchen and solar shower. This functions to fulfill the ethic of People Care and the principles of multiple functions and relative location. It aligns with the purpose of the garden zone as a functional extension of the home. This includes techniques from cold climate house design, and is a strategy to conserve energy, increase production and extend the growing season. Integral permaculture design comes from and connects back to all the main topics of the course : ethics, principles, design methods, patterns, techniques, strategies, zones, sectors, soil, trees, water, climate in general, our cool climate in particular, animals, and integral gardening methods. It also considers the human guild and any invisible structures like economics, governance, education and resilience which could also be addressed by the design.

Freely Available
www.permaculturedesign.ca

**PERMACULTURE WORKSHEET 106**

# DESIGN
## FINAL PROJECT

The final design presentation is short, no longer than 10 minutes. Share highlights and patterns instead of all the details so you can keep it clear, concise and connected.

Consider doing an ultimate permaculture design that allows you to apply more of permaculture without the constraints of you time, budget or resources. Also consider doing a practical design of something small that you could actually accomplish. You can do both the ultimate and the practical designs if you have time.

Like the map, the design project is less about finishing a design which will be an ongoing process, and more about getting started in an integral way and demonstrating that you can apply permaculture design to a garden, project, business, structure or relationship.

*"I believe the roots of Permaculture "sprout" from our deep desire to feel grounded. Permaculture allows us to be accountable, present and connected to our basic needs and surroundings in a way that modern society has taken away from us. It asks us to slow down and be an integral part of the process of life. At a cellular level, the collected memory of this process feels good to us and that connection and sense of purpose promotes increased productivity. We are a part of the ecological systems that are being designed and one of the indicators of success has to be that we "fit" and have not only our basic needs met by the system, but our deeper needs of community, purpose, and connection.*

*Start today, right now! Don't even finish reading this article! We have to quit talking about what we want to have happen and start making it happen. There is no perfect place or situation to start this work. Stop thinking you'll start when you get your land or find your community. Permaculture is not what we do once we find optimal conditions, Permaculture is the path to optimal conditions. Build, plant and act as if this is your one chance, and you will live a life with many rich chances for the choosing. Act like a perennial not an annual. Don't fool yourself for a second that this will not be hard work, even in the perfect conditions it will be, but we need systems to develop in every condition. Where you are right now, with the information you have, is the time and place to start. Match what you know to the scale of the project you undertake and dive in."*
- **Michael Becker** www.vimeo.com/gaiacraft/inspiringeducation

Freely Available
www.permaculturedesign.ca

# SOCIAL PERMACULTURE
## SOCIOCRACY AND DYNAMIC GOVERNANCE

### VALUES
- Effectiveness: Get things done
- Transparency: Everyone knows
- Equivalence: Fairness/ equality

### GOVERNING PRINCIPLES
- Consent decision making : decisions are made by consent not consensus.
- Circle organization : semi-autonomous self-governing groups, each of which has its own goals, and the responsibility to direct, operate and measure its own processes.
- Double Linking : An appointed representative of each working group (circle) participates with equal power in the governing group (circle) that oversees and supports their decision making processes and initiatives. Likewise an elected operational leader from the governing group (circle) participates in the working group. The governing group also sends an appointed representative to a higher level governing group, if one exists, and accepts an operational leader elected by that governing group as well.

### KEY BENEFITS
- Fast equivalent decision making process
- Objections are welcome and inform and evolve proposals
- Objections are validated in relation to the vision and shared aims
- Power is given to reason
- Roles are elected, not volunteered
- Full proposals are brought to meetings and are
- Solution based (every problem comes with at least 3 solutions)
- All decisions are time bound and re evaluated

### CHALLENGES
- Requires training of all participants to be effective
- Requires efficient and timely communication and facilitation

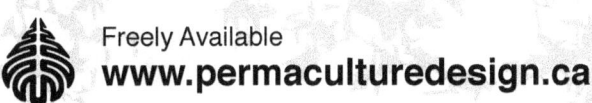

Freely Available
www.permaculturedesign.ca

# SOCIAL PERMACULTURE
## SOCIOCRACY AND DYNAMIC GOVERNANCE

### PROCESS
This is a formal decision making process. People will speak one at a time and in turn. If you are speaking out of turn, the facilitator will call 'point of process', this pauses the meeting and the proper protocol is restated before resuming. Everyone agrees to follow the sociocracy process and empowers the facilitator. People are asked to speak to the point and to consider if all proposals or discussions are in alignment with the mission, vision and aims. Facilitator fully participates in decision making process.

Step 1 - Convene the Circle reviewing mission, vision and aims
Step 2 - Present proposal
Step 3 - Ask Clarifying questions. this is not the time for opinions or ideas, only for questions to help understand the proposal more clearly. Questions are asked, one at a time, in order of the circle, and it goes around as many times as needed until there are no further questions.
Step 4 - Quick Reactions : options to discuss, amend, or refer to the relevant committee
Step 5 - Modify and re-present proposal if needed
Step 6 - Consent Round : consent, consent with concern, or objections and return to Step 5 or table proposal
Step 7 - Celebrate

### KEYS TO SUCCESS
- Full proposals are brought to meetings and are solution based
- Proposals are circulated and discussed before meetings

*"The Transition movement is a do-ocracy. People that do stuff get to decide what the organization is, where it's going, and what shape it takes. It's really the people who are doing stuff and driving the project on the ground who decide what is happening and what they need in order to support themselves. The role of decision makers is to support what communities are doing. It's not just to impose top down stuff, but to give communities the right support and space. There is a lot that can be done in terms of giving communities more say. Sometimes local governments come to us and say they want to start a Transition group. We tell them its not their role which is to support and enable this process but not to drive it. Transition comes from communities and is owned by those communities. The role of each tier of government is to support the one beneath it to deliver that work."*
- **Rob Hopkins** www.transitionnetwork.org

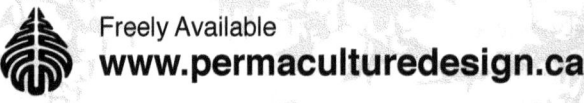

Freely Available
**www.permaculturedesign.ca**

# SOCIAL PERMACULTURE
## CONSENSUS DECISION MAKING

**VALUES**
- Inclusive
- Participatory
- Collaborative
- Agreement Seeking
- Cooperative

**KEY BENEFITS**
- Inclusive decisions
- Increased buy-in for implementation
- Strengthens group relationships

**CHALLENGES**
- Requires training of all participants to be effective
- Often more time consuming than other decision making methods

**PROCESS**
Facilitator is impartial and does not participate in the decision making process, they only drive it.
1. Discussion
2. Proposal
3. Vote : Consent, Consent with Concern, or Block
4. If yes, Consensus achieved
If the vote is no
5. Concerns are raised
6. Modification of Proposal
7. Vote : Consent, Consent with Concern, or Block
If blocked go back to step 5

**KEYS TO SUCCESS**
- Shared values and clear mission, vision, aims
- Compassionate communication
- Trust in collective wisdom

Freely Available
www.permaculturedesign.ca

# SOCIAL PERMACULTURE
## CONSENSUS DECISION MAKING

**QUAKER-BASED CONSENSUS**
- Values silence and active listening
- Encourages concise, relevant contributions to decision making process
- Concerns and information are shared until everyone is clear
- Ideas, solutions and decisions are associated with the group, no names are recorded
- Dissenting perspectives are integrated into the final decision
- Emphasizes that objections which block or lengthen process are only to be done when absolutely necessary
- Process continues until full consensus has been reached, no matter how long that takes

*"Permaculture is a communication tool to explain to people what we are doing and why we think its important. It's a way to think and communicate about all the different subjects that are required when moving back to the land or reindigenizing ourselves. I want to see a saner world with more people living and doing permaculture instead of just waiting for tomorrow. A lot of people think that they don't have enough money, information, or skills and so they wait. I don't think that's very valid, you can just start! There is always something you can do right now.*

*We need to think about being producers instead of consumers, so that every sustainable farm has products that are going out and not just taking care of themselves, but something to trade and barter with to create a new economy. It's important to continuing building models where people can see permaculture and how valuable it is. I want to get people to think globally about the possibilities, learning from analogue climates and using plants from around the world. If your food, resources and supplies came from your region, just like all people did throughout all time, what would that look like? What would it look like if you lived like it really mattered? Permaculture does not have to be a weekend thing, or just something to think about, you can just go do it. You don't need a lot of stuff, just determination, persistence and a little imagination. If you really want to live this way you can."*
- **Sam Bullock** www.permacultureportal.com

 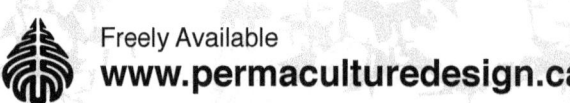

Freely Available
**www.permaculturedesign.ca**

**PERMACULTURE WORKSHEET 111**

# SOCIAL PERMACULTURE
## ORGANIZATIONAL STRUCTURES

Larry Santoyo says "play the game the way the game is played". In permaculture we seek to understand and interact with legal systems in order to protect ourselves and our assets while limiting unnecessary taxation.

### PPP : TRIPLE BOTTOM LINE
- People, Planet, Profit

### FOR PROFIT
- Private profit and assets

### NOT FOR PROFIT
- Benefits the public and assets held in trust and not privately owned

### CORPORATION
- Responsibility is held by the business, not by share holders

### SOCIAL ENTERPRISE
- Businesses owned by non-profits
- Uses commercial strategies and marketing to care for people and the planet
- Maximizes positive social, cultural and environmental impact while still generating income

### SOLE PROPRIETOR
- One person responsible for everything

### PARTNERSHIP
- Sharing responsibility with one other person

### CO-OPERATIVE
- Owned by members including consumers and producers who share in profits and benefits

### CREDIT UNION
- Member owned financial cooperative
- Dividends and profits distributed to members
- Offers investments and loans for local ethical projects
- Has accounts and credit cards backed by truly ethical investments

### SWARM
- is the collective behaviour of decentralized, self-organized systems

Freely Available
www.permaculturedesign.ca

# SOCIAL PERMACULTURE
## CONFLICT RESOLUTION

**CONSCIOUS COMMUNICATION**
- Listen actively, clarify, assess, speak
- Use direct communication
- Accept responsibility
- Pause before speaking
- Assume good intentions
- Attack the problem, not each other
- Be curious and test your assumptions by asking clarifying questions
- Don't take it personally
- Put yourself in the other persons shoes
- Show empathy and support
- Respond don't react, think before speaking
- Be solution minded and think cooperatively
- Look for common interests
- Speak from a loving place that considers the best interest of the collective
- Reflect back what you think you heard
- Acknowledge and affirm the person by saying comments like "I see you", " I hear you", "I know you need", "I know you feel"...
- If you are not being heard, after acknowledging the other persons words and feelings, restate your needs.

**COMPASSIONATE COMMUNICATION:**
- Creating a container
- Communication
- Reflection
- Resolution
- Celebration

Freely Available
www.permaculturedesign.ca

**PERMACULTURE WORKSHEET 113**

# SOCIAL PERMACULTURE
## CONFLICT RESOLUTION

**STEPS FOR NON-VIOLENT COMMUNICATION (NVC)**
- What do you observe?
- How are you feeling?
- What need is not being met?
- How could it be done differently in the future? (request)
- Be concrete and clear, describe the specific situation factually
- Share real emotions and take responsibility for how you feel using I statements like ; I feel happy, angry or sad.
- Address needs. What would make you feel better?

Example :
I notice that you play your music loudly late at night when this happens I feel restless and frustrated because I need to get a good rest as I wake up early. would it be possible for you to turn your music down after 11pm on nights when I have to be up early the next day?

*"Let us act as if we are part of nature's striving for the next evolutionary way to respond creatively to the recurring cycles of energy ascent and descent that characterize human history, and the more ancient history of Gaia, the living planet. Imagine that our descendants and our ancestors are watching us"*
- **David Holmgren** www.holmgren.com.au

Freely Available
www.permaculturedesign.ca

# SOCIAL PERMACULTURE
## OPEN SPACE TECHNOLOGY

A creative way for hosting meetings, conferences, and community building events. There is a specific purpose, but no formal agenda beyond the overall theme.

**GUIDING PRINCIPLES**

1. Whoever comes are the right people
2. Whenever it starts is the right time
3. Wherever it is, is the right place
4. Whatever happens is the only thing that could have, be prepared to be surprised!
5. When it's over, it's over
6. The law of 2 feet : At any time, anyone can use their two feet and go to a different discussion.

**PROCESS**

1. Opening Circle : The whole group decides on what topics will be discussed. After a brainstorm of topics, the group chooses the most relevant ones to be the focus of the discussions.
2. Facilitator explains principle of open space technology
3. There are multiple unfacilitated conversations are happening at the same time based on the chosen topics.
4. Closing Circle : comment and reflection

"*I would like to see a world where people live in harmony with nature and each other, a world with social justice and appreciation for our diversity as human beings of gender, race, culture and language. I would like to see a world which understands that diversity generates resilience in human systems the same way it does in ecosystems, and where science can open up and admit the possibility that everything around us has consciousness. I would like to see a world where science and magic converge, where a sense of deep interconnection with the natural world, human world, and with spirit is part of everything that we do.*"
- **Starhawk** www.starhawk.org

Freely Available
**www.permaculturedesign.ca**

# SOCIAL PERMACULTURE
## WORLD CAFE

A method for creating collaborative dialogue around questions that matter. It is based on the network pattern. It is a process of having multiple connected conversations at the same time which share collective knowledge and shape the future.

**GUIDING PRINCIPLES**

Set the Context :
- Have a purpose. What is the reason you are bringing everyone together?

Create Hospitable Space :
- Host at a location that is safe, comfortable and encourages creativity.

Explore Questions that Matter :
- Use questions that are relevant to the group.

Encourage Everyone's Contribution :
- Invite active participation.

Connect Diverse Perspectives :
- Allow for movement between tables to diversify thoughts, knowledge and ideas.

Listen Together for Patterns & Insights :
- Encourage people to actively listen to others. Document highlights of the conversation to help see emerging patterns.

Share Collective Discoveries :
- Present harvests to the larger group.

Freely Available
www.permaculturedesign.ca

# SOCIAL PERMACULTURE
## WORLD CAFE

### PROCESS
- Seat up to 5 people at tables or in conversation groups
- Set up at least three rounds of conversation, approximately 20 minutes each.
- Engage questions. You may use the same question multiple rounds of conversation. Alternatively you can pose different questions in each round, to build on and deepen the exploration.
- Encourage participants to write, doodle and draw key ideas on provided paper.
- Upon completing the initial round of conversation, you may ask one person to remain at the table as a "table host" for the next round, while the others travel to another table.
- For the last round, people can return to their first table to synthesize their discoveries, or they may travel to a new table.
- After at least three rounds of conversation, initiate a period of sharing discoveries and insights to the whole group.
www.worldcafe.com

*"Permaculture principles help us to design people systems and decision making methods as well as gardens, inviting us to connect better and be more sensible in our design. This can support community organization and education, creating networks and looking at the connections between things. In permaculture, people work where their interests and passions are, and each group has their own aims and purpose.*

*A simple step that any community can take to help create a better world is to give attention and care to their group dynamic and how they work together for change. Looking at the facilitation that is used, and how they can meet their purpose, goals and passion as a group without having challenges or conflict. Communities can begin by letting go of egos, feeling what the planet needs and what their group needs, and working in peace, harmony and co-creation together."*
- **Robin Clayfield** www.dynamicgroups.com.au

**Source Curriculum:** Bill Mollison, David Holmgren, Rosemary Morrow, Toby Hemenway, Robin Clayfield, Larry Santoyo, Michael Becker, Looby Macnamara, Scott Pittman, Geoff Lawton, Robyn Francis, Mark Lakeman, Patricia Michael, Starhawk, Bullock Brothers, Tom Ward, Jude Hobbs

**Envoy:** Delvin Solkinson www.visionarypermaculture.com

**Foundational Work :** Kym Chi www.gigglingchitree.com

**Gaiacraft Workbook Editing Team :** Delvin Solkinson, Kym Chi, Annaliese Hordern, Tamara Griffiths, Jacob Aman, Tes Tesla, Niki Hammond

**Design :** Sijay James www.onbeyondmetamedia.com

Freely Available
www.permaculturedesign.ca

# SOCIAL PERMACULTURE
## LAND FOR THE LANDLESS

There are many opportunities to have land to grow food for everyone. Here are alternatives including simply getting the right to use the property without ownership.

### KEY NOTES
- Land is a resource not a commodity
- Everyone has the right to land access for housing and food

### OXFAM MODEL
- Listings of who has land they will let people farm in exchange for food or rent, and who seeks land to farm on

### CITY FARM OR COMMUNITY GARDENS
- Marginal land in the city which is dedicated to allowing people to grow their own food and/or food for market

### CITY AS FARM
- Locate feral fruit trees and any food on public land
- Harvests from private land whose owners want to share with the community

### COMMUNITY SUPPORTED FARM
- A producer-consumer co-op run by and for families and people who want to farm in exchange for a share of the food produced

### COMMUNITY SUPPORTED AGRICULTURE (CSA)
- Local people pay up front at a reduced rate for a yearly supply of food, supporting farmers
- When they need it and taking on some of the risks if there is a natural disaster resulting in less or no food that year

### EMPLOYEE SUPPORTED AGRICULTURE
- Part of employees wages go to supporting a farm run by a business or other organization and employees get some of the food produced in exchange

### NEIGHBOURHOOD SUPPORTED AGRICULTURE
- Spin farming of private and public land, from lawns to parks

### LAND TRUSTS
- Land set aside privately or by the government which can never be resold and only used for farming to preserve cultural heritage

Freely Available
www.permaculturedesign.ca

# SOCIAL PERMACULTURE
## DESIGNERS CHECKLIST

Your permaculture design certification will enable you not only to use Permaculture Design in your own life and work but also to serve as both a consultant and designer for others. Often this will involve a site visit and analysis. You can do consultation and design for any workspace, development, project, process or set of relationships. We will focus here on land development and you can modify it to create a checklist for other types of consultation and design that would still benefit from an analysis using permaculture principles and concepts.

When you do a site analysis, depending upon the time accorded, you can work alone or with your clients to acquire specific information and answer design questions that will enable you to create a truly informed and intelligent consultation and design. Sometimes this analysis will lead to you doing a design, other times it will just be used as a consultation for the owners of the land, either way it will be a huge help.

Here are some things you may want to weave into your design consultation and site visit. Some of these things the client could prepare before you arrive and have ready.

### MAPS
- Acquire all existing maps (regional district, blueprints, google earth, etc.)
- Create a map of the property
- Learn about zones, codes, easements, recycling / waste pick up, neighbours, plants and animals in the community, invisible structures and invisible sectors
- Find out about the different local resources (good and services, allies and supporters)
- Seek out public land and parks, walking and biking trails, public transit and community centres

### HISTORY OF THE LAND
- Traditional patterns of plant use, agriculture and hunting
- Recent history of the land since it was first developed from unmanaged land
- Research knowledge through elders in the neighbourhood, libraries, public records and historical organizations

Freely Available
www.permaculturedesign.ca

**PERMACULTURE WORKSHEET**

# SOCIAL PERMACULTURE
## DESIGNERS CHECKLIST

**FEATURES**
- Landforms (major rocks, hills, elevation shifts, landmarks)
- Permanent buildings
- Roads
- Trails
- Fences
- Structures
- Topography, slope and aspect
- Views
- Location of plants, animals, insects, fungi and soil organisms as well as their food sources and habitat
- Access ways, roads and paths

**FLORA**
- Gardens
- Forests
- Lawns
- Functional plants

**FAUNA**
- Birds
- Mammals
- Reptiles
- Amphibians
- Insects
- Fish

**WATER**
- Supply : wells, aquifers, barrels, cisterns, ponds, springs
- Running water (streams, brooks)
- Aquaculture
- Salinity
- PH
- Oxygen levels
- Seasonal temperature ranges
- Drainage patterns

Freely Available
www.permaculturedesign.ca

**PERMACULTURE WORKSHEET 120**

# SOCIAL PERMACULTURE
## DESIGNERS CHECKLIST

**ELEMENTS**
- Note all elements, tools, resources or functional objects on the land
- Find the locations of any utility lines like gas, hydro, phone etc

**SOIL**
- Salinity
- PH
- Nutrient content
- Basic makeup (sand, humus, stone, minerals)
- Depth of hardpan or parent rock

**CLIMATE**
- Patterns of sun and shade
- Wind direction and speed range
- Seasonal sunrise and sunset times
- Seasonal rainfall
- Seasonal temperature range
- Frost free period
- Microclimates
- Zone analysis
- Sector analysis
- Localized microclimates with distinct temperatures, dryness or wetness, exposure to elements, soil types

**DESIGN GOALS**
- What new elements are wanted by the land stewards?
- What already existing elements are not wanted by the land stewards?
- What functions do the land stewards want fulfilled by the design?
- How can the land be organized to save energy? generate surplus?

Collaborate with the client to:
- Create beautiful documentation
- Outline the entire process of design, discovery, and application
- Create learning opportunities
- Stay organized with what has been done and what the plan is!
- Media can cater to the clients personal style and usability

Freely Available
www.permaculturedesign.ca

**PERMACULTURE WORKSHEET**

# SOCIAL PERMACULTURE
## DESIGNERS CHECKLIST

**CLIENT INTERVIEW**
- Discover needs and wants
- Create the initial relationship between you and client
- Set clear expectations
- Establish channels of communication
- Build confidence and authority
- Learn about the already existing relationships
- Discuss budget including for ongoing maintenance schedules
- Create statement of intent
- Learn what resources are already available (or are needed)
- Match complexity of plan and amount of upkeep needed with the available time and resources and lifestyle
- Listen and read between the lines for what clients need and what they have the time / resources / inspiration to actually do
- Keep in regular touch with client
- Send checklists / questions to client ahead of time
- Ensure a clear understanding of clients budgets and timelines and create appropriate project phasing
- Have a clear financial agreement about payment and timings of payment
- Value your time and charge the 'going rate' to make sure your work is valued

Any design consultation will just be the starting point for a longer mapping and design process. Help get people organized so they can continue this life-long process on their own and think about your relationships with your clients as long term where you may do yearly paid check ins to support with the systems feedback, client questions and support until the systems is fully functioning.

**Source Curriculum:** Bill Mollison, David Holmgren, Rosemary Morrow, Toby Hemenway, Robin Clayfield, Larry Santoyo, Michael Becker, Looby Macnamara, Scott Pittman, Geoff Lawton, Robyn Francis, Mark Lakeman, Patricia Michaels, Starhawk, Bullock Brothers, Tom Ward, Jude Hobbs

**Envoy:** Delvin Solkinson www.visionarypermaculture.com

**Foundational Work :** Kym Chi www.gigglingchitree.com

**Gaiacraft Workbook Editing Team :** Delvin Solkinson, Kym Chi, Annaliese Hordern, Tamara Griffiths, Jacob Aman, Tes Tesla, Niki Hammond

**Design :** Sijay James www.onbeyondmetamedia.com

Freely Available
www.permaculturedesign.ca

PERMACULTURE WORKSHEET 122

# OS PERMACULTURE
## PERMANOMICS

Permaculture design can evolve all kinds of relationships and systems of development. It applies to all spheres of our society.

Here are a few of the 'invisible structures' of society that permaculture can help to evolve

**PERMACULTURE ECONOMICS**

The new world of economics is about relocalizing the economy through the use of local trading currencies. A permaculture economy is about solving the needs of the local human and ecological community. By providing for more of our own needs locally, we can reduce the need to earn as much money, have more time to pursue our creative projects and family life while creating a thriving community based economy. Methods of exchange outside of the formal economy are meant to be complimentary to it, and not an alternative. They help to build trust amongst community members and create a more resilient economic system.

**WAYS TO MEET OUR NEEDS**
- Not spending
- Many small incomes
- Saving
- Income substitution
- Receive surplus
- Make our own stuff
- Upcycle
- Reduce energy needs and inputs of goods
- Spread your risk
- Diversify
- Use by-products
- Minimize maintenance
- Always have a back up
- Increase natural resources

Freely Available
www.permaculturedesign.ca

# OS PERMACULTURE
## PERMANOMICS

Currency can be looked at on a Yin - Yang Spectrum.

Yang Currencies work well in situations like : tax collection, competition, debt-based, quick profit, fear-based, interest (musical chairs), scarcity, treasure-hoarding, idealistic, exponential-curve pattern, long-distance trading

Yin Currencies work well in situations like : gift circles, cooperation, mutual-credit, long-term planning, trust-based, demurrage (negative interest rate), abundance, community-building, appropriate, realistic, sine-curve pattern

When designing a community currency make sure to have
- Constant Catalog Updates
- Active Matchmaker
- Transparent Accounting (digital?, paper vouchers?, tokens?, commodity-backed?, proxy currency?)
- Respect Gifts. Never monetize real gift economies, and allow natural transition to real gift economy.
- Play with real live example of CC design using a participant's project

## COMMUNITY CURRENCY
- Promotes relocalization and energy cycling
- Supports local people providing goods and services
- Encourages ethical business practices
- Matches requests and offers and provide a large catalogue of local goods and services that the currency can be exchanged between

## KEY NOTES
- Consent : there is no compulsion to trade
- Disclosure : information about balances is available to all members
- No interest on accounts
- It takes 100 people to support 100 people

**Source Curriculum:** Bruno Vernier www.permametrics.org
**Envoy:** Delvin Solkinson www.visionarypermaculture.com
**Foundational Work :** Kym Chi www.gigglingchitree.com
**Gaiacraft Workbook Editing Team :** Delvin Solkinson, Kym Chi, Annaliese Hordern, Tamara Griffiths, Jacob Aman, Tes Tesla, Niki Hammond
**Design :** Sijay James www.onbeyondmetamedia.com

Freely Available
**www.permaculturedesign.ca**

# OS PERMACULTURE
## PERMANOMICS

**8 FORMS OF CAPITAL**
- Material Capital, Financial Capital, Intellectual Capital, Spiritual Capital, Social Capital, Living Capital, Cultural Capital, Experiential Capital

**GREEN / ETHICAL ECONOMICS**
- Considers all environmental and social costs associated with a product, service or development

**CRADLE TO CRADLE ECONOMICS**
- Considers the real costs of extraction, processing, production, distribution, use and reuse or disposal of goods and services

**INFORMAL ECONOMY**
- Barter, Trade of Swap
- Work Parties : groups of 5 or more alternating working between their properties

**SEMI-FORMAL ECONOMY**
- Time Bank:  hour for hour exchange of services
- L.E.T.S. : local employment and trading system which involves creating our own money

**HUI**
- Pool money and pay back with interest
- Invest in fundamental functions of the community that are needing support
- People present business plans that address real need in the community
- Money gets paid back to everyone
- From the community for the community

**INFORMAL ECONOMY**
- Barter, Trade or Swap
- Work Parties : groups of 5 or more alternating working between their properties
- Craigs list : online listing of goods and services offered for free or for sale by individuals
- Skills bank : a registry of who does what in your neighbourhood

Freely Available
www.permaculturedesign.ca

# OS PERMACULTURE
## PERMANOMICS

### NEW ECONOMY
- Create a pattern literate community with local control of money flow and use of conscious local trading currencies
- Investing in things that are needed in the real economy and abundant economic design
- Real economies simply solve the needs of the local community
- Divestment : withdrawing money from unethical investments

### SLOW MONEY
- Long term profits with slow return on investment
- Community and environmental benefit is seen as an important part of the profit
- Relocalized, ethical investment

### RIGHT-LIVELIHOOD
- Making a living doing activities that support and benefit human and ecological communities

### RESILIENCE
- The ability of a community to provide for its own goods, services and needs locally as well as adapt, recover and respond to any kind of crisis or disaster that may strike

### GLEANING
- Gathering unused or left over food and resources

### SLOW FOOD
- Local, seasonal and artisanal
- Includes traditional techniques and cultural preservation
- Cooking on demand, convivial eating (slowly), locavore
- Encourages social interactions

### GREEN DIRECTORY
- An inventory of the resources in a local community
- Ethical buyers guide to support people to become conscious consumers
- Shows openings for new businesses, goods or services that may be needed
- If produced annually it can show how the community is progressing in becoming more

Freely Available
www.permaculturedesign.ca

# OS PERMACULTURE
## BIOREGIONALISM

**BIOREGIONALISM**
A political, cultural, and ecological system or set of views based on naturally defined areas called bioregions. Bioregions are defined through physical and environmental features, including watershed boundaries and soil and terrain characteristics. Bioregionalism stresses that the determination of a bioregion is also a cultural phenomenon, and emphasizes local populations, knowledge, and solutions. We want to create more opportunity for local support be created in your bioregion?

"*In the last few decades permaculture has focused on land care of gardens, farms and woodlands which are very tangible and easy to demonstrate. What's emerging now is personal and social permaculture which show how the same design principles and sense of hope and responsibility can lead us to the transformation of our inner world. It starts from ourselves and our relationships, then moves out into our communities, nations and international systems where the transformation can happen on a very big scale. It's usually the people dynamics that that limit us and holds us back from Earth care. When we start addressing the limits of people, whether its in communication or international politics, then we can really create big shifts in what happens. We have to go deeper, looking at the paradigms our culture is operating under which result in the destruction of our ecosystems. Paradigm shifts that can enable us to do Earth repair and care is where permaculture is heading.*

*There is a very short time frame that politicians are thinking about. Permaculture can expand our timeframe to see outside of the box of our community and nation, recognizing that everything is connected and that all the consequences of our actions have ripples that come back to us. This invites more responsibility, not just for the people or the system that we are governing, but for a wider system. Through taking responsibility, we bring the ethics into action. With this approach there will be more sensible decisions that work for people and the other beings we inhabit the planet with.*"
- **Looby Macnamara** www.loobymacnamara.com

**Source Curriculum:** Bill Mollison, Scott Pittman, Larry Santoyo, David Holmgren, Rosemary Morrow, Toby Hemenway, Robin Clayfield, Michael Becker, Looby Macnamara, Mark Lakeman, Starhawk

**Envoy:** Delvin Solkinson www.visionarypermaculture.com

**Foundational Work :** Kym Chi www.gigglingchitree.com

**Gaiacraft Workbook Editing Team :** Delvin Solkinson, Kym Chi, Annaliese Hordern, Tamara Griffiths, Jacob Aman, Tes Tesla, Niki Hammond

**Design :** Sijay James www.onbeyondmetamedia.com

Freely Available
**www.permaculturedesign.ca**

# OS PERMACULTURE
## PLACEMAKING

**VILLAGES AND NEIGHBOURHOOD DESIGN**
- Distributed energy supply (energy, food, gardens, water on every house)
- Site houses in clearings for protection
- Farms and woodlands surround settlements
- Woodland protected roads and rivers
- Maximize freedom for individuals
- Opportunities for responsibility, learning and incomes
- Ecological controls shared : cleaning and saving water, building soil, animals controlled
- Aim self sufficient, decentralized, independent areas throughout the country

**GOALS**
- Local transport
- Dispersed ecosystems
- Local economy, markets, products
- Long term forests
- Wildlife corridors
- Open space
- Zero waste
- Share resources

**SUBURBAN DESIGN**

**OBJECTIVES**
- Abundant, Restored, Beautiful

**STRATEGIES**
- Co-operation
- Small clean industries
- Independence
- Work-nets
- Group planning

**GOALS**
- Harvesting resources (dumps, unused food)
- Total waste recycling and all renewable energy
- All water harvested and cleaned
- Get animals and insects back
- Have fun

  Freely Available
www.permaculturedesign.ca

**PERMACULTURE WORKSHEET 128**

# OS PERMACULTURE
## PLACEMAKING

*"When we look each other in the eye without fear, the village is ignited within us."*
- Mark Lakeman

**ARCHETYPES OF A VILLAGE**

- Boundaries/ form/ edges (enhance, activate and inspire)
- Gateways/ portals (welcomes people into the space)
- Village heart (the place where the community all comes together)
- Pathway/ journey (pathways through and around)
- Nodes of activity (sanctuaries, seating areas, play spaces, workshops etc..)
- Places of memory or sacred places (the physical fabric of our lives, including art, stories, gardens, altars etc..)

Public spaces are for :
- Reconnecting
- Rejoining
- Coming together
- Sharing

Things that support thriving community :
- Participation and stewardship
- Gathering places
- Safety
- Food security
- Healthy eating and active living
- Open spaces
- History and education
- Wildlife corridors and native plantings
- Visual beauty

Freely Available
www.permaculturedesign.ca

# OS PERMACULTURE
## PLACEMAKING

This Worksheet has taken information and sampled text directly from
**City Repair's : Placemaking Guidebook**
Creative Community Building in the Public Right of Way
www.cityrepair.org

Here you will find a summary primer of some information found in that wonderful text. This is not intended to be a substitute for reading it yourself, if you are inspired by what you see here, we recommend you purchase this life changing book directly from City Repair to get the full transmission.

The City Repair community facilitates the creation of public gathering places and events that invite people to connect with the people and places around them. City Repair helps people physically change their neighbourhoods to be more community-oriented, ecologically sustainable and simply more beautiful. It is an organized group action that educates and inspires communities and individuals to creatively transform the places where they live and take active, direct roles in re-inhabiting neighbourhoods. At the heart of this work is the localization of culture, economy and decision making through placemaking and community participation. City Repair facilitates artistic and ecologically-oriented placemaking through projects that honor the interconnection of human communities and the natural world.

Placemaking is the act of creating a shared vision based on a community's needs and assets, culture and history, local climate and topography. It is as much about psychological ownership and reclamation of space as it is about physically building a place. As the process of creating a community place progresses, people develop deeper relationships and more momentum to create together because they have discovered a way to directly change the world in which they live. Placemaking is based on the belief that everyone is a designer and a good design should serve social interaction and cultural development.

Intersection repair is the citizen-led transformation of a street intersection into a public square. Its takes a crossing of pathways, the historical place of gathering, and turns it back from a place to move through into a place to stay.

Freely Available
www.permaculturedesign.ca

# OS PERMACULTURE
## PLACEMAKING

**COMMUNITY BUILDING : GETTING TO KNOW YOUR NEIGHBOURS**

At the heart of Placemaking is human relationships. Opening up meaningful relationships with your neighbours and community is a deep intention of this evolving movement. Some ways this can be done is :
- Say hello and introduce yourself to your neighbours when you see them around
- Start conversations with your neighbours about anything!
- Create public spaces to meet in and enable direct connections
- Reach out to your neighbours and offer to help them in small ways or give them extra fruits and vegetables from your garden
- Invite your neighbours to tea or a visioning walk around the neighbourhood to talk about who they are and share a bit about yourself
- Create a neighbourhood or street newsletter
- Collect pets names and make a pet map
- Set up a skill or tool sharing network, plant share system, babysitting/play group
- Host potlucks
- Invite an organization to offer workshop in a relevant skill like bike safety, street trees, weed id, intersection repair, tool sharing
- Create an asset map for your neighbourhood including the strengths and resources available including people and their skills, structures, natural resources, institutions, businesses, organizations, physical or invisible structures that can contribute to the community
- Develop a walking / biking tour for your neighbourhood
- Set up a community garden
- Knock and talk : just go up to your neighbours door and introduce yourself
- Learn more about the block by asking neighbours who they already know and what has happened in the past
- Make flier greetings and invitations to mail to neighbours you don't see around
- Build phone and email trees to enable communication between your neighbours
- Set up a community kiosk to post information and facilitate communication
- Ask neighbours what kind of community they want to live in and what they might like to see that could be built to improve the place
- Learn about what events, gatherings and classes are offered by your neighbours and in your community and attend some of them
- Build partnerships with schools, non-profits, government groups, businesses and individuals in the community
- Set up formal neighbourhood meetings about community issues, projects and potentials
- Produce free events, celebrations, games, block parties, actions and intersection repair projects that include your neighbours

  Freely Available
www.permaculturedesign.ca

# OS PERMACULTURE
## PLACEMAKING

**PLACEMAKING PROCESS : OUTREACH AND INVOLVEMENT**
- Do research on City Repair initiatives and read City Repair's Placemaking Guidebook
- Google City Repair videos
- Start documenting as much of process as possible
- Set up a community garden and garden collectively
- Set up a seed bank and seed saving network
- Learn more about the neighbourhood or block by asking neighbours who they already know and what has happened in the past
- Start documenting as much of process as possible
- Open dialogues
- Begin relationship building through socials and community meet-ups
- Form a core group to help guide the process
- Build partnerships with local people, businesses, organizations, schools, and government groups
- Make an Asset Map : an inventory of the strengths and gifts, both tangible and intangible, of the people and places that make up your community
- Deepen dialogues about possibilities and create a collective decision making process
- Observe the design space and openly brainstorm possibilities
- Involve as many people as possible from the neighbourhood into a collective visioning process
- Talk to people who did not attend meetings to allow them still to be involved
- Form a core group (neighbourhood association) of those wanting to dedicate more time and support this process in its creation and maintenance
- Create a flexible plan for schedules and goals regarding meet ups, doing design charrettes, work parties, maintenance plans and organizational structure including time, energy, supplies and costs estimates
- Develop a specific vision and mission statement
- Co-create goals that are relatively easy to achieve to build group momentum and empower the process
- Facilitate lots of opportunities for feedback

Freely Available
www.permaculturedesign.ca

# OS PERMACULTURE
## PLACEMAKING

- Include local government in the process of finalizing the design
- Partner with local businesses community groups and organizations that may be able to help
- Be sure to note any bylaws, codes or other guidelines
- Begin fundraising if needed
- Consider getting signed support from all directly adjacent neighbours as well as 80 % of the neighbours within two blocks of the site (one person per household)
- Make a green community map of your neighbourhood *including boundaries, pathways, gathering places, signs, monuments, sites of interest and social centres
- Make the magic happen
- Create publicity to share the inspiration and encourage others to do similar projects
- Celebrate the accomplishment with a block party or social
- Reflect on the process
- Steward the new community place
- Keep the momentum going with socials, events and new community initiatives
- Set up a Book club, phone tree or email list serve
- Write down list of volunteers and participants
- Develop a walking/biking tour for the neighbourhood including sites of interest
- Do neighbourhood mapping including gates, pathways, defining features, signs, places, monuments, and centers

"Placemaking is a reflection of the vision and the participation of people in a place. It's not a thing that someone external can design, it's something that has to emerge from the ground where people are. The way it relates to permaculture is that permaculture is concerned with things that from a holistic perspective. You want functions to stack, you want to engender relational networks. You want to multiply your fruitfulness with him a maximum of grace and a minimum of effort. This is the sort of stuff that everybody is concerned with. Nobody really wants to work harder than they need to, they really do want to be known and heard, and they want to have a relationship with their place their story and the people around them. They want to be able to comprehend it. They want to be able to share it! So placemaking is a reflection of permaculture, its the integration of everything. When people are in a place, they start to interact, they communicate, they want to be effective communicators and that means that they are going to be facilitating, they are going to be listening, they are going to be making decisions. Permaculture enables people to get excited, I think thats the reason I get up in the morning. Its like this challenge we are facing as a global commmunity and all local communities is the greatest most unifying crisis we have ever had in the history of the world, if world peace ever had a chance its right now."
- **Mark Lakeman** www.cityrepair.org

Freely Available
**www.permaculturedesign.ca**

**PERMACULTURE WORKSHEET**

# OS PERMACULTURE
## PLACEMAKING

**PLACEMAKING FUNCTIONS**
- Builds community
- Reclaims public spaces
- Turns spaces into places
- Creates ecologically sustainable, community-centred neighbourhoods
- Allows people to meet freely without having to spend more or feel they need to move on
- Greens the local neighbourhood
- Addresses social and environmental concerns
- Habitat building for animals and birds
- Creates beauty
- Slows down traffic
- Encourages other neighbourhood projects
- Is super fun
- Reduces crime
- Increases property value
- Brings neighbours together
- Re-indigenizes our cities, towns and villages
- Opens up dialogues about local collective visioning the future
- Helps people get to know neighbours
- Initiates a community design process
- Promotes biking and walking
- Create connections between local schools, businesses, organizations, government and neighbours
- Supports reskilling and skill building
- Addresses social isolation
- Attracts families and conscious people to the neighbourhood
- Creates community resilience
- Increase communication and interaction between neighbours
- Inspires participation and cooperation in *community issues and projects
- Cultivates neighbourhood identity, *culture and economy
- Lowers crime rates

Jan Semenza introduces two important concepts around placemaking:
- Develops Community Capacity which is defined as "characteristics of communities that affect their ability to identify, mobilize and address social and public health problems"
- Builds Social Capital "The norms and social relations embedded in the social structure of society that enable people to coordinate action to achieve desired goals"

Freely Available
www.permaculturedesign.ca

**PERMACULTURE WORKSHEET 134**

# OS PERMACULTURE
## PLACEMAKING

**INTERSECTION REPAIR ARCHETYPES**
- Public art installation
- Traffic circle
- Library
- Free box
- Cafe
- Tea house (mobile or fixed)
- Community gardens
- Cob oven
- Sitting areas + cob benches
- Tool lending library
- Mural
- Information kiosk / communication station
- Multi use space
- Farm gate stand
- Produce sharing station
- Sidewalk chalk dispensary
- Chalk board
- Bike rack
- Bike paths
- Table
- Signage
- Lighting
- Water feature
- Garbage / recycling station / compost (if properly maintained)
- Stage
- Pathways
- Mandala
- Pocket park
- Food forest
- Nature strip
- Transform street intersections into public squares
- Bulletins to information and communicate about current events
- Tile mosaics
- Cob
- Rammed earth
- Strawbale
- Cord wood
- Earth bags 2

Freely Available
www.permaculturedesign.ca

# OS PERMACULTURE
## PLACEMAKING

- Mushroom logs
- Greenhouses
- Chicken runs
- Greywater system
- Healing garden
- Compost station
- Worm farm
- Skate park
- Bioswales
- Ecological art by gutters and downpipes
- Planter boxes
- Grass couches
- Fruit and nut trees
- Native food shrubs and perennials
- Interpretative maps
- Community green maps
- Tea garden
- Green roofs
- Solar fountain
- Outdoor classroom
- Benches, tables and unconventional seating areas
- Depave areas for gardens or gathering places
- Establish a bike or car share co-op
- Block party
- Babysitting networks
- Co-op gardening / spin farming
- Happy and connected neighbours

*"Placemaking is ecological. People want to pay attention to the direction of the wind and know where the light is happening. They want to capture that light and rain and turn their so called waste into a resource. A place is memorable, beautiful, functional and resilient over time because it integrates all these different considerations. Designing is a means to engender relationships between people. Creating things that are intentional and permanent in public space is literally creating a sense of commons where before there was only a void. These things stands in shining contrast to the product driven landscape all around them, they are a poem and a metaphor embodying sustainability. Thousands of people pass by every day, and somewhere deep inside, or maybe right close to the surface, realize they have never thought about that before. The idea is to open them up."* - **Mark Lakeman** www.cityrepair.org

Freely Available
www.permaculturedesign.ca

**PERMACULTURE WORKSHEET**

# OS PERMACULTURE
## PLACEMAKING

Inspired by City Repair in Portland, Gaiacraft has launched :
**Village Repair : Design Maquettes for Small Towns and Villages**
www.villagerepair.org

The Village Repair branch of Gaiacraft is a local grassroots initiative growing in the mossy cedar rainforests of Mt. Elphinstone, British Columbia. In the Heart Gardens and surrounding downtown core of our coastal village, a unique community comes together to build foundations for a regenerative future. Here we can see social permaculture vignettes intended to inspire creative placemaking in small towns and villages around the world. Village Repair focuses on creating relationships, gathering places and habitat that promotes healthy interactions between people, animals, birds, reptiles, insects, plants, fungi and all other living and non-living links in the ecological community. As an activated Social Permaculture program and Transition Initiative, Village Repair hopes to inspire communities to redesign their own neighbourhoods into thriving, abundant and diverse ecosystems which support the web of life for all living and non-living things.

The localization of culture, economy and decision making is the foundation for a sustainable future.

*"It's really simple. This is our home. We live in these patterns that tell us little about ourselves. Instead of realizing that this is our home, we are living in a reality that is literally an invasive set of patterns. We have been swept up by a huge wave of colonial and cultural disruption of extreme violence. I think the great revelation of placemaking is to realize that the earth is our home. When you look at any geomorphic settlement where people are adapting to the land and building out of what is available, it becomes an expression of their earth based intelligence.*

*Community is built best through using our bodies together, sweating, singing songs, handing things to each other and carrying things. As we create together, it reflects us all."*
- **Mark Lakeman** www.cityrepair.org

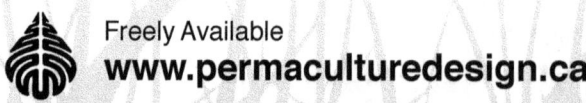

Freely Available
www.permaculturedesign.ca

**PERMACULTURE WORKSHEET** 137

# OS PERMACULTURE
## DESIGN FOR RESILIENCE

*"No disaster can be handled alone."* - Rosemary Morrow.

**WHAT IS RESILIENCE**
- Being adaptable in changing times.
- Having numerous support systems in place with back ups.
- Design that buffers from extreme weather events and human induced emergencies.
- Thinking preventatively.
- Creating trust and building community.
- Sustaining ourselves, each other and the planet.
- Using whatever you have, wherever you are to take action.

**WHAT IS DISASTER**
- A disaster is something that effects the entire community and requires a community response.
- Disaster is dramatic and life changing, it takes people by surprise and often has long term consequences.
- Causes can be natural or man made.

**STEPS TO RESILIENCE**
Emergency prevention, preparedness and response

Stage 1- Awareness
GOALS: build community and community trust.
STEPS: come together, create a disaster profile for your local area.

Stage 2- Prepare & Network
GOALS: continue to build community, have equity in contribution, build resilience, learn the needs of the local area and its vulnerabilities.
STEPS: asset mapping, prevention and preparation.

Stage 3- Endure
GOALS: be coherent and forward looking, seek models and indicators for regeneration, vision with long term thinking, replace what was, with what could be, use appropriate technology.
STEP: respond.

Stage 4- Regenerate
GOAL: make it better than it was together, strengthen areas of vulnerability
STEPS: renew and reflect.

Freely Available
www.permaculturedesign.ca

**PERMACULTURE WORKSHEET 138**

# OS PERMACULTURE
## DESIGN FOR RESILIENCE

**COMMUNITY BUILDING**
- The community has the knowledge, skills and resources needed to create true resilience.
- How would you get a community to start developing solutions and actions for disaster?
- What are the steps needed to take disaster training to your community or council?
- E.A.S.E: Engage, Acknowledge, Share and Earn trust.

**DISASTER PROFILE**
Reviewing the history of disasters in an area helps us to see the patterns of events over time and their impacts. This enables us to plan and prepare better for future and more importantly create preventative measures to avoid occurrences in the first place. When creating a profile we research and document:
- Type of disaster
- Cause ( was it human or natural caused? )
- Frequency
- Time to onset
- Duration and recovery time
- Scope
- Degree of destruction
- Controllability
- Predictability
- Secondary Disasters
- Indicators
- Risk assessment
- Resources

**NEEDS AND ASSET MAPPING**
Observe and document:
- Skills and resources you have
- Skills and resources available in your community
- Gaps or needs in your local area
- Demographics of your area with acute attention to children, seniors and those with special needs.

Freely Available
www.permaculturedesign.ca

# OS PERMACULTURE
## DESIGN FOR RESILIENCE

### PREVENTION AND LONG TERM PLANNING
How can Permaculture help?
One of the key functions of Permaculture Design is creating resilience.
Looking at your disaster profiles, create a design with prevention in mind that considers:
- Water catchment, treatment, storage and overflow.
- Soil health
- Regeneration of the landscape
- Fire, wind, flood, drought, animal, pest, toxins and disease protection
- Food and medicine supply
- Needs of the community and economy
- Back ups for all systems and when possible, back ups for your back ups

### KEY NOTES
- The earth's conditions must be met before we can be self sufficient.
- Self sufficiency is only achieved in community and when communities needs are met.
- Observe patterns to details; pay attention to what is happening globally and how it effects us locally.
- Watershed management in rural areas is a must.

### ACTIONS TO BUILD RESILIENCY
- Work at a street or community level.
- Work with groups.
- Create a local directory of skills and distribute.
- Plan big to include your whole community with nodes and networks that can connect and reach everyone when needed
- Build local food networks.
- Train up trainers to build in resilience into every level of the system.
- Host events and workshops that build trust, develop skills and strengthen networks.
- Promote community resiliency at community events and festivals.

Freely Available
www.permaculturedesign.ca

# OS PERMACULTURE
## DESIGN FOR RESILIENCE

**PREPARATION**
Short term needs & priorities
Visible Structures

Use checklists for supplies and evacuation plan.

**SUPPLIES**
- Community contact list highlighting children, seniors and those with special needs
- Evacuation bag (backpack for everyone)
- Radio or walky talky, if possible a phone with solar charger for communications
- Food - 6 wk supply : 16kg - 30 kg/ person/ month of grain
- Water - 6 wk supply : 3 L of water / person / day
- Water filter or cleaning tablets and water bottle
- First aid
- Flashlights with battery back up and candles with waterproof matches
- Identification and medical information in a waterproof ziplock bag
- Cooking supplies
- Energy, heat and light
- Blankets
- Tools and hardware
- Tarps and ropes
- Tents if possible
- Note book and pencil
- Compass, topographic map, signals
- Building supplies
- Seeds for regeneration
- If possible, resources - permaculture texts, wild skills and SAS books

Freely Available
www.permaculturedesign.ca

**PERMACULTURE WORKSHEET 141**

# OS PERMACULTURE
## DESIGN FOR RESILIENCE

**INVISIBLE STRUCTURES**
- Create teams

Consider :
- Communications
- First Aid
- Transportation
- Food storage and preservation
- Cooking
- Shelter and building
- Waste and sanitation
- Energy
- Water
- Counselling, conflict resolution and vibe watcher
- Safety
- Childcare and activities
- Education and training

**STAY OR EVACUATE**

Stay:
- How can you create a refuge?
- What actions will be required?
- Consider communications for fire, flood, pandemic, nuclear and storm

Evacuate:
- When will you evacuate?
- How long might you have to evacuate for?
- Who will have to go?
- Where will you go?
- What will you take?
- What will you leave?
- How will you communicate?

*"We cannot wait around anymore for resources and permission before we can start, the revolution we seek has to be based on actions we can take wherever we are with whatever we have right now."*
- **Mark Lakeman** www.cityrepair.org

  Freely Available
www.permaculturedesign.ca

**PERMACULTURE WORKSHEET 142**

# OS PERMACULTURE
## DESIGN FOR RESILIENCE

**RESPONSE DURING A DISASTER:**

**ACTION**
- What are you doing?
- What are the priorities?
- What are the roles and responsibilities?
- Make sure you are including everyone.
- Have activities for people to do

**SUPPLIES**
- Kits for evacuating or staying
- Checklists
- Appropriate technology

**FEEDBACK**
- How is it working?
- Vibe watch and conflict resolution
- People care and self care

**ASSESSMENT**
- What are the gaps?
- What are the challenges?

**RECOVERY**
- Ensure that the disaster is over
- Address priorities like injuries, illnesses and unsafe structures
- Consider security, warm and dry bedding, antiseptic, hot water when possible, sanitation, equal distribution of supplies, hygiene and clear access
- Check on those in need

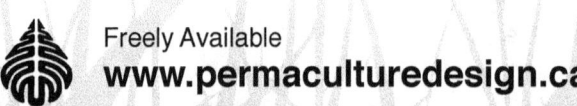

Freely Available
www.permaculturedesign.ca

# OS PERMACULTURE
## DESIGN FOR RESILIENCE

**REGENERATE**

Be transparent and as public as possible about the disaster so that more resources will be available to you.

Meet and decide;
- Priorities
- Roles and responsibilities
- How to make it better than before
- How to redesign and rebuild with prevention and resiliency in mind
- What resources are available?
- Where can you attain donations?
- Where can you contribute?

**REFLECT**
- Encourage talking about what happened and share feelings
- Review what went well with the plan what didn't work and what you would do differently?

*"There are two populations of greatest need. One is those who are caught up in the world of capitalism to a degree that they are prisoners of it. They are so trapped that they can't see a way out. This group often includes decision makers. The other population is those who don't know that there are choices or how to start. These can be refugees or those in poor places, people who have the right to know.*

*Permaculture offers an environment restored and a quality of life that populations in need cannot imagine exists. Some cannot make choices because of poverty, others cannot make choices because they are caught in a trap of materialism that seems indispensable to them. Permaculture offers them some leisure, creativity, decision making, autonomy and community."*
- **Rosemary Morrow** www.bluemountainspermacultureinstitute.com.au

**Source Curriculum:** Rosemary Morrow, Kym Chi, Dana Wilson, Annaliese Hordern, Chris Walker, Susie Lees, Ben Walter

**Envoy:** Delvin Solkinson www.visionarypermaculture.com

**Foundational Work :** Kym Chi www.gigglingchitree.com

**Gaiacraft Workbook Editing Team :** Delvin Solkinson, Kym Chi, Annaliese Hordern, Tamara Griffiths, Jacob Aman, Tes Tesla, Niki Hammond

**Design :** Sijay James www.onbeyondmetamedia.com

Freely Available
**www.permaculturedesign.ca**

**PERMACULTURE WORKSHEET 144**

# DESIGN FUTURES
## POST-PDC PERMACULTURE

**NEXT STEPS**

While people completing PDCs (Permaculture Design Certificates) come from all walks of life, ages and backgrounds, they have three things in common:
- They are usually concerned about the state of the world, both with ecosystems and social levels and tend to have an above-average understanding on the predicaments we face
- They are usually proactive and empowering people who like to get things done
- They are eager to start "doing something" with what they have learned but do not necessarily have a plan (or even a vision) of what this may look like

What comes after a PDC will be hugely influenced by:
- Your vision/goals
- Your skills and experience in whatever you were doing before the PDC
- Your current assets and liabilities ( in all aspects )
- Your community landscape.

**VISIONS AND GOALS**

- As in any Permaculture project, all starts with a vision: what do you want for the world, your community, your household, your life? What do the world, your community, your household and you need?
You may have a vision/goal of:
- Becoming a Permaculture activist. Promoting Permaculture in your community and engaging people so they can learn, apply its principles and start projects
- Becoming a Permaculture teacher. Teach PDCs and eventually advanced programs such as Social Permaculture, Transition or Permaculture Teachers Training
- Becoming a Mentor for those going through the Permaculture Diploma program certification
- Becoming a Permaculture Consultant/Designer who helps others to visualize and implement projects in their lives and communities. What type of consultant might you be? You may coach at social/inner level, be a career coach for the Right Livelihood, or coach people on creating full self-reliant systems such as edible gardens/forests, energy systems, etc...
- Becoming a Permaculture "doer'. Beyond planning, you want to support people to implement and actually build the structures for the projects they dream
- Using Permaculture in your life and household with no further goals for now beyond improving yourself and your ecological footprint

Knowing what your dreams are will guide the next steps.

Freely Available
www.permaculturedesign.ca

**PERMACULTURE WORKSHEET 145**

# DESIGN FUTURES
## POST-PDC PERMACULTURE

**SKILLS AND EXPERIENCE**
Your skills and experience, more if you were good at what you are doing and enjoy it, may be a foundation of whatever comes next in your life after the PDC. You might not abandon a landscape just because it is not a perfect fit for what you want, you can use design so it can be more functional.
- Do you have a background in trades? That will surely help with hands-on projects.
- Do you have a background in social services or community work? That will be a great asset for community based projects!
- What about a creative background such as business, IT, engineering, policeman, nurse, musician?
- This may mean you may need to work a bit more in developing an "edge" (or not) depending on what Permaculture Design means for you in your future plans

**ASSETS AND LIABILITIES**
- Assets and liabilities may come in many shapes and sizes, from both inner and outer sources
- Do you have dependents?
- Does your family support your Permaculture dreams?
- Are you emotionally and spiritually strong enough to change your life right now?
- Can you overcome financial challenges?
- Do you have a mortgage and bills to pay?
- Are there other people depending on your current income?
- Can you overcome health challenges?
- Are you young and healthy, both physically and emotionally to embark yourself in this new adventure?
- Both assets and liabilities are very personal and yours may include many others not quoted here.
- Having certain assets, such as access to land to start a garden or time to plan and implement all your changes, can help with the starting and maintaining momentum, but they are not all you need.
- Having liabilities may slow you down or become a challenge. This means it will be a bit more difficult for you and you may need to be more creative on how you use and work with what you have.
Same as we work matching needs, functions, products, services and inherent characteristics to get a resilient and self-reliant system in our Permaculture design, knowing where you stand will allow you to "design" your path after the PDC.

Freely Available
www.permaculturedesign.ca

**PERMACULTURE WORKSHEET 146**

# DESIGN FUTURES
## POST-PDC PERMACULTURE

**COMMUNITY LANDSCAPE**

Your community landscape is like the different sectors and elements in your Permaculture design. Some sectors and elements may restrict what you can do, such as community by-laws, regulations and even current neighbours attitude. Some may support your vision, such as an existent Transition group or community hub. Permaculture teaches us that flows of energy can be captured and stored, used up, channeled or deviated or blocked. Knowing what you already have in your community or household may provide ideas of where to go and how to address that. It will also tell you where the needs and gaps are and where the points you can use as leverage might be.

Your next steps:
Once you know where you stand you have a much better understanding of what you need to do. For some, the road ahead may mean years of engaging in projects, more reading and even formal education. For others, it may mean continue doing what you love, just adding a Permaculture twist.

*"I would like to see a world where the Earth is restored in such a way that natural systems are understood and respected for what they do for us, and we are seen as givers and not takers. I would like to see a world where natural systems intrude profoundly into urban and agricultural spaces, and where people are totally engaged in these processes."*
- **Rosemary Morrow** www.bluemountainspermacultureinstitute.com.au

*"I think about permaculture in a broader sense of efficiency and the interconnectedness of different elements in the system. When we are working, installing and designing, we consider how it's going to effect whole area. We think about all the functions of the system and how they interrelate, using that as a teaching tool for many of the people who come through our site to participate in the different programs offered here. I am in service to my garden. All my fruit trees are calling to me to pick and prune. I wander around, observing and interacting, looking at plant health, overall system efficiency, diseases, drought, infertility, crowding, and airflow. I can analyze the trees overall health and function in the system by just eating the fruit that particular year. I also care for ducks and chickens and deal with predation from deer, squirrels, slugs and snails. My function is sensing, being aware, and discussing with other people living on the land what is doing really well and why, what is suffering and why, as well as what direction to take this in."* - **Doug Bullock** www.permacultureportal.com

Freely Available
www.permaculturedesign.ca

**PERMACULTURE WORKSHEET**

# DESIGN FUTURES
## POST-PDC PERMACULTURE

Here are some suggestions that may work for almost anybody:
- Register to local and global networks. This will allow others to meet and connect with you and you will have more people to consult and invite to your projects.
- Start small and slow. Apply what you have learned at home. No matter what your dreams are, if you don't walk your talk people may not trust working with you
- Continue learning. Either through a second Permaculture Design Course (PDC) with a different teacher, an Advanced Permaculture Design Course (APDC) or a Mentorship Program towards a Diploma.
- Read more and watch videos. What opportunities exist for you locally?
- Apply what you learn. Engage in projects at home, work and community level. Join working parties, meetings and planning / designing projects
- Offer your consulting, teaching and designing services for free or as exchange to family, friends or colleagues and document all you do. A portfolio will help you if your plans are aligned with teaching, designing or consulting.
- Specialize. Although Permaculture is about systems thinking, you don't need to know it all. You can specialize in something you love, such as soil, or building resilience or social Permaculture. The advantages of specializing is that you'll be offering something to the party instead of competing with others.
- Visit permaculture sites and explore hands on opportunities to volunteer, WWOOF, intern or apprentice in working permaculture systems.
- Just do it! There is nothing more disempowering that lingering and dragging.

**Source Curriculum:** Silvia Di Blasio www.mainstreampermaculture.com

**Envoy:** Delvin Solkinson www.visionarypermaculture.com

**Foundational Work :** Kym Chi www.gigglingchitree.com

**Gaiacraft Workbook Editing Team :** Delvin Solkinson, Kym Chi, Annaliese Hordern, Tamara Griffiths, Jacob Aman, Tes Tesla, Niki Hammond

**Design :** Sijay James www.onbeyondmetamedia.com

Freely Available
**www.permaculturedesign.ca**

# DESIGN FUTURES
## NEXT LEVEL EDUCATION

This was assembled by Delvin Solkinson across three Permaculture Diplomas, a Masters Degree and Doctoral Degree in Permaculture Education. It was gleaned from courses taken including 6 PDCs, 9 Teacher Trainings and 11 Advanced Permaculture courses.

It lists elements, strategies and components that may lead to more success in teaching permaculture to people of all ages and educational backgrounds. Mostly this material came from teacher trainings with Bill Mollison, Geoff Lawton, Robin Clayfield, Robyn Francis, Rosemary Morrow, Looby Macnamara, Jude Hobbs, Tom Ward, Douglas and Sam Bullock, Michael Becker, Dave Boehnlein, Scott Pittman and Larry Santoyo.

As with everything it in this workbook, it has been edited and upgraded brilliantly by the Gaiacraft Team including : Kym Chi, Annaliese Hordern, Tamara Griffiths, Jacob Aman, Tes Tesla, Niki Hammond

Michael Becker notes that "we don't need a new curriculum, we just need a new delivery system and way of assembling the information"

**WHAT TO DO AT START**
- Check classroom, check list, tech, visibility, seating, comfort, setup
- Include everyone
- Check in
- Create a learning space and safe container
- Introduce what is going to happen with an orientation, schedule, time table
- Engage and inspire, light the spark of interest
- Intentions, responsibilities, aims, hopes and expectations
- Housekeeping, logistics, practicalities, food, fulfilling needs, orientation (micro and macro), site tour, venues, awareness of surroundings, hazards, privacy, health and safety, first aid
- Course culture, guidelines, rules
- Welcome each person, by name, and let them know you are happy they are there
- Share resources available
- Posted time table that can be tweaked or rearranged
- Establish privacy, health and safety, first aid and identify certified first aid people

Freely Available
www.permaculturedesign.ca

**PERMACULTURE WORKSHEET 149**

# DESIGN FUTURES
## NEXT LEVEL EDUCATION

**TEACHING ETHICS**
- Give information which is accurate, clear and verifiable
- Delivery which is succinct, non-jargon, respectful
- Learnings welcomed as knowledgable, skilled, aware, to be listened to
- Practice fidelity to care of people
- These Ethics
come from core beliefs
make students feel valued
share transparency
give accountability

**GOOD TEACHER QUALITIES**
- Demonstrate moral value and beliefs
- Project empathy (compassion)
- Communicate clearly and simply
- Are authentic, say what they believe
- Are trustworthy
- Present a model students can identify with
- Have passion for what they teach

**BEHAVIOURS OF EFFECTIVE TEACHERS**
- Present to learners needs
- Encourage student participation
- Hand over the pen / chalk
- Don't need to know / tell everything and say if don't know
- Speak 30% time / let others speak
- Keep attention on students
- Explain clearly
- Monitor learning
- Allow expertise to be revealed

Freely Available
www.permaculturedesign.ca

PERMACULTURE WORKSHEET 150

# DESIGN FUTURES
## NEXT LEVEL EDUCATION

**PRINCIPLES OF THE CLASSROOM**
- Keep personal issues out of the classroom
- Know the subject well
- Like and respect students
- Seek natural authority not power
- Taking responsibility for safety and knowledge
- Remember your class is watching
- Always enable students to contribute if they can
- Learners want Respect, Enthusiasm, Knowledge, Safety and Trust

"Permaculture education is providing a model by having no boundaries and enabling fields of study to splinter off according to interest, potential and need. Examples include the ecovillage network as well as school gardens which fly off from permaculture, floating away like lovely little sections of seeds which can start germinating elsewhere. Instead of turning us all into brain surgeons, accountants or carpenters, permaculture can produce a diversity of people who go out into society to enrich it. Permaculture people can be of any age or gender because everyone is equally capable of absorbing the materials. It's an open system with no boundaries, no leader, and no board of education. We are getting back to people centered education."
- **Rosemary Morrow** www.bluemountainspermacultureinstitute.com.au

"What permaculture helps us to do is to think differently. We can start to apply the permaculture thinking to find the solutions any problem, enabling and empowering people. Rather than giving people the solutions, permaculture empowers people to find their own solutions and take responsibility for their own learning."
- **Looby Macnamara** www.loobymacnamara.com

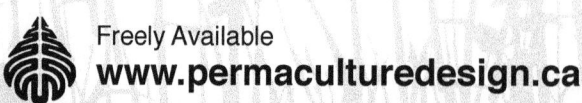

Freely Available
www.permaculturedesign.ca

# DESIGN FUTURES
## NEXT LEVEL EDUCATION

**KEY NOTES FOR SUCCESS**
- Small groups
- Good, well established site
- Better posters
- Practiced at drawing diagrams
- Keep it entertaining
- Creatively develop peoples' own ideas for things in their lives
- Bringing the curriculum into absolute relevance for people
- Dynamic, changing, and engaging workshops with creative presentations
- Catering to students with your language, attention and learning styles
- Having energetic awareness of the students
- Empathy with students needs
- Well planned in advance
- Arrive early to set up the learning environment
- Creates discussion
- Practical and relevant
- Experiential
- Local and bioregionally relevant
- Cross-platform media and mediums
- Includes peer teaching and learning
- Welcome students to be involved in opportunities after the course is over, to stay connected
- Encourage cooperation and networking
- If you ask questions, leave people time to answer them
- Look in people's eyes
- Create a living classroom
- Use Blackboards
- Engage the senses
- Make students part of the process
- Root everything in the direct experience of the instructor
- From the start, build upon the participants previous knowledge
- Starting at the beginning
- Keep it moving
- Keep it fun
- Keep it relevant
- Making connections and observations
- Empowering people by helping them to learn by themselves
- Shifting mediums and modalities

Freely Available
www.permaculturedesign.ca

**PERMACULTURE WORKSHEET 152**

# DESIGN FUTURES
## NEXT LEVEL EDUCATION

- Empowering the students to help teach
- Being a part of the team
- Teaching by example
- Teaching what you know
- Foster and nurture interest
- See, touch, feel, taste what is being talked about, recreate the feeling to help with memory
- Hands on planting activities give empowerment, self-esteem and health
- Say what you feel
- Be part of a food cycle (growing and eating in the garden)
- Remember to breathe
- Make sure creature comforts handled
- Have great food and an adaptable chef
- Relating information back after a debrief
- Chunks spread across time
- Have multiple exercises to select from depending on the group, seasonality, location and resources available
- Hone specific skills
- Networking with teachers and include guest presenters
- Showing students that systems are connected
- Break down of misbelief that things exist separately in disconnected ways, casting out the disempowering premise that things are not connected
- Include a multidisciplinary process
- Tools made in activities can be a starting point for the next activity
- Model team teaching
- Stick with the schedule
- Wait
- Don't be tied to a specific outcome
- Trust the process
- Make jokes
- Tell relevant short stories to illustrate a point
- Give book and film lists
- Use positive reinforcement
- Laugh out loud
- Have a plan, and a back up plan
- Use technology ensuring you have all the cables and tech to make it work
- Share research
- Be excited about your subject
- Say 'I dont know'

Freely Available
www.permaculturedesign.ca

# DESIGN FUTURES
## NEXT LEVEL EDUCATION

- Clarification of group process
- Solicit feedback
- Mix of educational styles
- Role model
- Comparative studies
- Learn from models that work
- Take field trips and nature walks
- Dispel myths
- Offer advice
- Build networks
- Choose your own groups
- Smile/breathe
- Group resume
- Meet in circles
- Guided and supported with notes and handouts
- Utilize Multi-colour note taking
- Encourage notebooks
- Include learning buddies and teams
- Student facilitation
- Change schedule as needed
- Incorporate yoga and stretching
- Constant evaluation process was adapted into a living curriculum
- Teaching transparencies / moments to share hidden process
- Participants learn how to healthily critique each other and give critical feedback
- Teachers provide constant evaluation and feedback to students
- Lots of research material made available in hard copy and online
- Socratic method, asking questions, talking less than 50% of the time
- Focus on outcomes competence in participants in core topics and skills
- Masking tape more environmental than other tapes
- Teaching is an exchange not a delivery
- Model punctuality as a teacher
- Ask "what isn't clear' instead of 'is this clear' (makes people think)
- Make learning easy
- Guiding group to their desired outcome without any attachment to outcome
- Playing expert and giving a transmission
- Directing group to specific outcome
- Quote little known fun facts and jaw dropping statistics
- Have attachment to the content

Freely Available
www.permaculturedesign.ca

# DESIGN FUTURES
## NEXT LEVEL EDUCATION

- Show leadership
- If something is not right, address it immediately
- Guide group learning process

**LEARNING TECHNIQUES**
- Take notes
- Move around
- Evaluate your learning style
- Discus topics
- Take photographs
- Journal
- Look for examples and applications in your own life
- Teach those around you
- Make worksheets
- Journal about learning moments and teaching moments
- Every person being heard, no person talking too much, no leaders in groups

"There are many ways that permaculture can help people. Some are very practical and concrete like helping people grow food, find systems that can regenerate a local economy, and produce for their needs in ways that are regenerating the environment around them instead of destroying it. Looby Macnamara said is that "Permaculture is a shift in our way of thinking". This is the core, a shift from thinking about separate isolated things to thinking about relationships, systems and flows. Understanding that everything is in relationship is a very deep spiritual shift. This is also a shift that science is going through at a deep level, from the old mechanistic model of the universe to a string theory and new physics understanding. When you look for the smallest piece of stuff, you find is there is no stuff, there is only relationships made of strings, harmonies and probabilities. If we can integrate this understanding, then we can reimagine our technologies, science, industries, and ways of doing things, bringing them back to being in harmony with the natural world."
- **Starhawk** www.starhawk.org

Freely Available
**www.permaculturedesign.ca**

# DESIGN FUTURES
## NEXT LEVEL EDUCATION

**TEACHING TECHNIQUES**
- Circles
- Games
- Short brainstorm
- Processing tools
- Images
- Stories
- Storytelling
- Voice modulation
- Individual projects
- Letters to self
- Photograph learning cards
- Readings
- Resource lists
- Utilize Calendars
- Group tasks
- End in silence
- Songs
- Initiatives
- Case Studies
- Discussions reflected on paper pad (mind map)
- Trust building
- Empowering students to teach
- Inner permaculture
- Mixing lecture with discussion
- Best of yesterday
- Movement : encourage people to stretch in class
- 10 minutes chunks for attention
- Repetition
- One liner hooks
- Diagrams and pictures
- Posters
- Utilize learning and teaching tools
- After lunch video or easy dialogue
- Take it slow
- Relate theory to real life situations
- Ask questions to involve and engage students
- Break into small groups

Freely Available
www.permaculturedesign.ca

# DESIGN FUTURES
## NEXT LEVEL EDUCATION

- Cultivate teaching voice with inflections and gestures
- Change it up with vocal variety
- Encourage feedback
- Self evaluation
- Relax and calm the nerves
- Careful of stiffness that comes from reading with notes
- Watch eyes and body language
- Careful of sexual innuendo
- Ask the class a question and answer it
- Using humor and seriousness
- Drawing on the board
- Using gentleness and warmth as well as strength and intensity
- Share from a diverse repertoire
- Note facial expressions
- Keep energy up and be animated at times
- Move around the room
- Sit on floor to share in a chill way
- Sit on low chair to tell a quiet story
- Sit on high chair or on stage to speak with authority
- Standing or sitting straight on to communicate directly on same level
- Balance of formality of lecture with interactive teaching
- Design how and when you do things
- Note what indicates you did it right
- Questions put into a cue
- Drawing with one line
- Write on board in all caps
- When writing on board talk at the same pace that letters and pictures are coming up
- Allow other people to correct you if you are wrong
- Watch out for repetitive things that are said
- Go live with other teachers through skype
- Develop a toolkit different techniques and delivery systems
- Creative use of story
- Be performative to engage students
- Importance of icebreakers
- Toys and props
- Two stories, two funnies, two analogies, two tearjerkers / serious moments
- Check in with students to get feedback

Freely Available
www.permaculturedesign.ca

# DESIGN FUTURES
## NEXT LEVEL EDUCATION

- Opening up feedback of students
- Pinboard process (posting different ideas / brainstorms on a board as an interactive creative process)
- Make group agreements
- Recapitulations of each day or days before
- Dynamic styles that change regularly and engage
- Catering to students needs: language, attention, and learning styles
- Inviting and creating discussion
- Black boards and coloured chalk
- Rooting: direct experience of the instructor and student
- Keep it moving and inspirational
- Create opportunities for self reflection
- Empowering: help to teach or co teach
- Teach what you know and are passionate about
- Networking teachers: guest presenters and different perspectives
- Showing students how systems are connected and how
- Revisiting information through different approaches
- Vary voice tone
- Pace all communications
- Tell imaginary stories
- Glue processes
- Energizers or light and lively activities
- Relaxation
- Revision
- Check in
- Brain games
- Icebreakers
- Grouping process
- Evaluation processes
- Completion processes
- Talk about learning moments
- Familiarizing with the environment
- Relaxation
- Positive learning expectation
- Goal-vision
- Take in the big picture
- Ask questions
- Chunking

Freely Available
www.permaculturedesign.ca

# DESIGN FUTURES
## NEXT LEVEL EDUCATION

- How do you learn
- Use your senses
- Play with it
- Put it together
- Cater to all eight intelligences : musical, visual, verbal, logical, kinaesthetic, interpersonal, interpersonal, naturalistic, existential
- Wild design
- Self test
- Talk with others
- Do it
- Learn from our mistakes
- Remember
- Frequent breaks
- Sleep on it
- Be happy
- Take notes
- Importance of giving everyone the chance to talk
- Always use short, easily answered questions
- Have students speak in front of class in a simple, easy way at the start to give them confidence to speak and participate in the course later
- Ask students to declare their intentions so you can cater the course best
- Never comment on people's spelling or grammar
- For blackboard work use clear, large writing; first write then turn around and talk
- If people bring up irrelevant info, have a parking board that they can write stories, questions and such on to feel that they are heard
- Set up learning agreements:
- Importance of monitoring students the whole time to assess understanding
- Suggestions for group agreements that avoid "don'ts" by giving "do's"
- Importance of sharing where you have come from and where you are going
- Set tone and objectives for the course
- Trust building exercises
- Modelling healthy learning habits
- Remember there are at least 6 ways to do anything, keep it dynamic

Freely Available
www.permaculturedesign.ca

# DESIGN FUTURES
## NEXT LEVEL EDUCATION

**PRESENTATION METHODS**
- How safe are learners to speak and contribute
- How comfortable are students
- Are your needs being met
- Is it a good learning environment
- Are you getting knowledge
- Are you getting enthusiasm

**TEACHING TOOLS**
- Visible
- Has an impact
- Multiple functions
- Simple
- Appropriate
- Everything and everyone can be a teaching tool support

**GAMES**
- Need to cooperative
- Need to be inclusive
- Need to match a purpose (e.g. to raise energy, drop energy)
- Some cultures can't touch
- Note mobility and abilities of group

**DESIGN CHARRETTES**
- Fast track design process
- Different groups with minimal design outlines
- An exercise for design mind
- Design for stronger relationship between the people and the landscape
- Team based
- Study design approaches, particularly which perspective to bring needs and opportunities from
- Topical approach (based on specific topic)
- Locational or spatial approach (based on specific sites)
- What is the best way to communicate information
- Group project includes working groups, resolving conflict, process of designing and working with clients

Freely Available
www.permaculturedesign.ca

# DESIGN FUTURES
## NEXT LEVEL EDUCATION

**TEACHING PERMACULTURE**
- Jump into the deep end and you simply have to swim
- You will find success in just getting out there
- Discover your own style
- Observing your own weaknesses and evolving personal learning based on integrating observations and feedback
- Importance to just keep taking steps forward
- Get confident and comfortable
- Importance to respect other people's cultures
- Give yourself a few days to observe new culture before teaching in it
- Careful of initiating eye contact and hand shaking or hugs
- Start by being more respectful and formal and take cues for what is acceptable and when it's ok to be more casual
- Instead of singling out students, giving general examples to the whole class particularly about what not to do or to clarify rules that are broken
- Keep things simple and don't get too personal, particularly about relationships and sexuality
- Observation and measurement is part of every lesson
- Building knowledge through observation and deduction (drawing conclusions)
- Analysis (include pattern), synthesize (include pattern)
- Bring together people skills and earth skills

**LEARNING RETENTION**
Percentage of information retained from learning modalities
- Reading 10%
- Hearing 20%
- Seeing and Hearing 50%
- Speaking 80%
- Speaking and Doing 90%

Freely Available
www.permaculturedesign.ca

# DESIGN FUTURES
## NEXT LEVEL EDUCATION

**TEACHING QUALITIES**
- Conversational style
- Know students strengths and weaknesses
- Support and motivate
- Give reasons and possible alternatives
- Offer reassurance
- Make praise personal (e.g. initiative / independence / critical thought / creativity / perseverance / willingness to learn)
- Make info relevant / enticing
- Assist success
- Teacher must know material
- Never punish, blame or patronize
- Respect for students (tolerance + acceptance)
- Need be passionate
- Effective communication
- Relevant
- Organized and clear
- Take breaks
- Quality and quantity
- Open to change
- Specific needs of learners
- Meets course outcomes
- Empowering
- Resources to support knowledge
- Use hooks
- Literacy, language and numeracy (L.L. and N)
- Timely
- Well planned
- Motivate learners
- Creativity and variety
- Recognize prior learning
- Using graphics to illustrate whole systems
- Include Gardening experiences
- Ask clarifying questions
- Yell
- Whisper
- If you are going to lecture, be loud and clear

Freely Available
www.permaculturedesign.ca

PERMACULTURE WORKSHEET 162

# DESIGN FUTURES
## NEXT LEVEL EDUCATION

**TEACHING MANAGEMENT**
- Time keeping
- Keeping on topic
- Organize physical resources
- Setting the objective
- Set and enforce ground rules
- People manager
- Time management
- Boundary management
- Class environment
- Energy levels

**COMMUNICATION**
- Utilize diverse delivery styles
- Clear, concise, connected
- Impart their subject
- Good public speaking skills
- Exuberant energy
- 30 seconds of FaceTime with each student each day

**ADULT LEARNERS**
- Know things. Find out what they already know
- Like to be treated as individuals, learn names
- Some, despite appearances, are not confident, treat them gently
- Prefer cooperation to competition, use cooperative methods like clumping
- Learn better when participating, involve them
- When feeling safe like to be challenged, try difficult ideas and questions
- Need relevance
- Want to feel security, need acceptance and tolerance
- Recognition, give respect
- Understanding the purpose of a lesson or information, give examples
- Teacher is a helper not a director

Freely Available
www.permaculturedesign.ca

# DESIGN FUTURES
## NEXT LEVEL EDUCATION

**CREATIVE PROCESSES**
- Brainstorm
- Mindmap
- Story telling
- Modelling
- Sandpit
- Roleplay
- Chalk drawing
- Treasure hunt
- Quizzes
- Visualizations
- Card games
- Pinboard
- Sticky carpet
- Affirmations
- Plus, minus, interesting (PMI)
- Making and doing
- Crosswords
- Buzz pairs
- Fuzzy felt
- Board games
- Sensory journey
- Ritual
- Puppetry
- Jigsaw puzzle
- SWOT (Strength Weakness Opportunities & Threats)
- Problem solving
- Open space
- World cafe

Freely Available
www.permaculturedesign.ca

PERMACULTURE WORKSHEET 164

# DESIGN FUTURES
## NEXT LEVEL EDUCATION

**GLUE PROCESSES**
- Facilitator intro
- Participant intros
- Name games
- Site orientation
- Housekeeping (including first aid kit)
- Group goals and guidelines
- Check ins
- Energizers
- Grounding processes
- Breaks
- Meal times
- Brain exercises
- Speed dating
- Revision
- Curtain up
- Trust games
- Relaxations
- Completions
- Evaluation
- Celebration

*"The future of permaculture, I suppose, is as it's past-mythic. We will one day hear of permaculture courses, of permaculture teachers, even permaculture practices, but we will speak of it no more. Not just because of how embarrassing it might be to think that once we had to take a class and pontificate about a reasonable grasp of the obvious. That's it forgotten, mythic. Permaculture will be so obvious so de-centralized, so incorporated into every day thought- that it will never be spoken of again..."*
- **Larry Santoyo** www.permacultureacademy.com

Freely Available
www.permaculturedesign.ca

**PERMACULTURE WORKSHEET 165**

# DESIGN FUTURES
## NEXT LEVEL EDUCATION

**TEACHING PROCESSES**
- Self paced learning
- Active listening and feedback
- Anecdotal
- Individual research
- Written activities
- Workplace practice
- Chalk and talk
- Tea breaks
- Discussions
- Demonstrations
- Small group work
- Charts and posters
- Coaching
- Hands on
- Case studies
- Questionaires
- Lecturing
- Anecdotal story telling
- Field trip
- Reading
- Electronic
- Mapping
- Debates
- Simulation
- Design exercise
- Problem based tasks
- Thinking skills exercises
- Using different facilitators and jumping between processes builds in breaks
- Keep learning session to 10 - 20 minutes
- Create hooks for learning using interesting information, memorable experiences, humour and excitement

Freely Available
www.permaculturedesign.ca

**PERMACULTURE WORKSHEET 166**

# DESIGN FUTURES
## POST-PDC PERMACULTURE

**PEDAGOGY OF TEACHING**
- Accept that you are vulnerable
- Stay in the body
- Stand and deliver
- Breath
- Task-oriented
- Teach in your own
- Disregard insecure inner chatter
- Look at people and engage the room
- Being honest
- Importance of journaling
- Sage on the stage
- Immersive
- Multigenerational
- Love what you are doing and show that to students
- Be true
- Be able to say you don't know
- Try to go to highest generalization
- Instead of education : transfer of knowledge
- Instead of growing food : providing nutrition to your family

"*I believe that the best outcome future of Permaculture lies within the concept of Right Livelihood. We have a commercial capitalistic model in place that has tremendous capacity for harm. Right now, all too often, people's self-worth is directly related to their earnings. This system arises from a lack of connection to place, people and environment. Permaculture is the link to re-connect us to those things in a meaningful way that could also return values of craftsmanship, local variation, moderation and community. Permaculture is a path to living richly within the means of the ecological system we reside in for an indefinite time period. If people really understood what that means the idea of wealth could change completely from nodes to whole system thought. We have to get past the idea of sustainability, sustainability is not the end game we are after. There are all kinds of horrible things out there I don't want to see sustained! Permaculture as a design tool seeks to maximize the productive yield while continually increasing and protecting the base capacity of the system. Only once we see our true role to protect and increase the base capacity of the system can we move beyond the idea of sustainability.*"
- **Michael Becker** www.vimeo.com/gaiacraft/inspiringeducation

Freely Available
www.permaculturedesign.ca

# DESIGN FUTURES
## NEXT LEVEL EDUCATION

**CONSIDERATIONS**
- Time management
- Introducing group
- Use functional models
- Integrate ethics and principles
- Reference to what is there
- Work towards goals
- Identifying client interest and commitment
- Refer to real possibility of design implementation
- Include seasonal variation
- How plants, animals and elements used in functional way
- Creating habitat
- Utilizing and adapting microclimate
- Look at role of people in the design
- Talk about physical and invisible structures
- How are you capitalizing on what is already there
- How things are connected together holistically
- Multifunctionality
- Practical and affordable design ideas
- Use of graphics
- Use of color, design and art
- Photos
- Scale
- What was what was appreciated
- Speaking slowly and clearly
- Giving overview and summary
- Overall site design
- Flows of paths and driveways
- Application of zones and sectors to design
- Clear function and purpose
- Breaking project down into manageable details
- Sharing highlights and key details without too much detail
- Mention process of designing with successes and failures
- Is this solving problems?
- Evidence of site visits and mapping
- Evidence of research
- Identifying leverage points
- Are you colouring outside the lines and doing something creative and unique?

Freely Available
www.permaculturedesign.ca

# DESIGN FUTURES
## NEXT LEVEL EDUCATION

- Water systems and catchment
- Energy assessment
- Trees
- Soil
- Can the property generate income and participate economically in the community?
- Show big picture
- Bringing out different possibilities
- What would be the best support for this project
- Identify relationship between strengths and weaknesses
- How the design fulfills needs of people, animals and plants
- Which principles were used
- How are the ethics are fulfilled
- How unused elements can get put into functional uses
- Explore more dynamic follow up
- Have students practice nano teaching, short teaching segment with debrief
- Make public apologies
- Include the story of permaculture, how Bill Mollison spent 2 years observing nature and asked why are not we not building everything like a forest? self maintaining, forest is model for perennial system,
- Make sure every person is heard, no person talking too much, no leaders in groups
- Key to internalize and teach third ethic, share surplus to need
- Stacking, write question down and if its not addressed bring it up later
- Outcomes, competence in participants in core topics and skills (sketch out paddock or identify a key line - not make compost)
- There are two resources : people and earth
- What must people be able to do know or do to be able to become Permaculturalists? Look at a landscape or a community or town - design and repair
- Cultivate people skills
- Observation and measurement is part of every lesson, building knowledge through observation and deduction (drawing conclusions)
(eg. learn slope, observe slope then deduce specifics about slope)
Analysis (include pattern)
Synthesize (include pattern)
- Cultivate Earth skills
- Ethics and principles
- Water (too much, too little, climactic factors)
- How to understand climate and its elements (radiation, wind, water)

   Freely Available
www.permaculturedesign.ca

# DESIGN FUTURES
## NEXT LEVEL EDUCATION

- Microclimates, the units of design (do not design on a climate level, we are designing to microclimate level : slope, aspect, vegetation, water, structures)
- Must be able to design to and create microclimates
- Forests, structure and function, windbreaks, plants and animals
- Patterns
- Site analysis skills happen alongside earth skills
- Brings together people skills and earth skills
- Analyse home site with map (catch and store, microclimates)
- Group project includes working groups, resolving conflict, process of designing and working with clients
- Social Permaculture
- Bioregion, bioregional analysis, designing neighbourhoods and towns, land tenure, legal structures, ethical money
- Swarming and divestment, social movements, how information passes through communities
- Disaster, aquaculture, pest management, wildlife encouragement
- Pin point people who have something unique to bring to Permaculture

"*Permaculture is the future, alive and active now in a time of change on our Beautiful planet. Already Permaculture supports people and nations across the globe to live better, take more personal responsibility for our lives and support and share with others to create a better world. The change grows, day by day, garden by garden, course by course, spreading through personal interactions and a knowing that Permaculture is one positive solution that holds the seeds for the new world.*"
- **David Holmgren** www.holmgren.com.au

Freely Available
www.permaculturedesign.ca

**PERMACULTURE WORKSHEET 170**

# DESIGN FUTURES
## NEXT LEVEL EDUCATION

**New PDC topics to add**
- Creeks and river cleaning, restitution of a creek line, restoration of remnant systems (get there quicker and better)
- Coastal restoration / coastal permaculture

Delta peoples ; Amazon delta, Ganges, Bangladesh, Holland (1/3 of the world lives on deltas)
Brackish and salt water systems, gardens and islands floated on reeds
What would Permaculture do with ocean rise?
Expand on island Permaculture
- Permaculture for refugee camps, for trauma zones, war zones, disease areas, orphanages, design for disaster expansion
- Performing arts as method with strategies and techniques
- Emphasis on people in media, money and community development or exploring non land based permaculture
- Redistribution of wealth, ethical opportunities to tithe
- Social Permaculture

*"The present courses we now teach in small groups need rethinking because the world is changing so quickly. The situation is grave and we must take on refugees, increasing desertification and floods with climate change and special endangered ecosystems such as islands, low coasts and deltas. Permaculture must reach forward to a more difficult future through planning new ecological towns, cities and villages and retrofit others. Permaculture has the concepts, ideas and constructs to be able to do it. We have a world system which is too stuck on economics. Permaculture has to step up to shantytowns and to the fact that 500 people a day are arriving in Berlin. Permaculture has to grow faster. We have to go beyond small groups of people learning on courses by stretching the syllabus and skilling ourselves. We must create swarm movements - after all, we really are one. We are also a clever, innovative and diverse community. We are on the side of Life."*
- **Rosemary Morrow** www.bluemountainspermacultureinstitute.com.au

Freely Available
www.permaculturedesign.ca

**PERMACULTURE WORKSHEET**

# DESIGN FUTURES
## NEXT LEVEL EDUCATION

**Australian Quaker Kerrie O'Reagan Teaching Song**

I sit on the hill and I look at a bee
The bee is the bee and I am me
But I am the bee and the bee is me
Not other but together we are one.

"*The future of permaculture pays attention to personal and social permaculture while bringing in fair shares. On the personal permaculture level, it's about breaking down the paradigms of our culture that we live within and operate from. By identifying for ourselves how we can make change and engage with our own responsibility and sense of hope, we can move forward using our passions and talents. On the social permaculture level, it's about breaking down the paradigms of competition, being able to work together in small groups, in large groups and in communities.*

*There is a bigger scale of things that needs to happen around fair shares and engaging people in the majority world. There are many people who are vulnerable and don't have the resources that we have. Permaculture looks to how we can shift the scale, so there is not such a huge disparity between those who have so much, and those who have so little. It starts with doing that in our own lives, breaking down the scarcity and fear mindset, enabling us to do more sharing. The future of permaculture gives voice to everyone in the world. It gives the capacity for everyone to make change, to step up to contribute in caring for the Earth and each other.*"
- **Looby Macnamara** www.loobymacnamara.com

**Source Curriculum:** Bill Mollison, David Holmgren, Rosemary Morrow, Toby Hemenway, Robin Clayfield, Larry Santoyo, Michael Becker, Looby Macnamara, Scott Pittman, Geoff Lawton, Robyn Francis, Mark Lakeman, Patricia Michael, Starhawk, Bullock Brothers, Tom Ward, Jude Hobbs

**Envoy:** Delvin Solkinson www.visionarypermaculture.com

**Foundational Work :** Kym Chi www.gigglingchitree.com

**Gaiacraft Workbook Editing Team :** Delvin Solkinson, Kym Chi, Annaliese Hordern, Tamara Griffiths, Jacob Aman, Tes Tesla, Niki Hammond

**Design :** Sijay James www.onbeyondmetamedia.com

Freely Available
www.permaculturedesign.ca

**PERMACULTURE WORKSHEET 172**

# MEDICINE MAKING
## WILDCRAFTING PRINCIPLES

**Protect and Regenerate Landscapes**
Never wildcraft in an old growth forest, around old growth trees or on conservation land. Remember these areas are for visiting, observing and learning.

**Make it Beautiful**
Leave no trace or leave a regenerative trace! Pick up waste. Before you gather anything, observe the terrain and consider how you can leave the least amount of impact.

**Law of Return**
- Only take what you need or 30% of what is there (whichever is less).
- Harvest in such a way that makes the plant grow better with increased productivity.
- When possible, take just the branches, foliage or flowers, leaving the remaining plant in tact. In rare cases, when the whole plant is needed, the seeds should be left behind.
- Taking just the top third of the plant is a good rule of thumb.
- When harvesting roots and rhizomes, make sure to gather at the best time for the plant
(usually during dormancy) and replant root and rhizome pieces to propagate.

**Care of Future**
- Only collect from areas that are abundant. Learn which plants not to gather, including endangered, over harvested and scarce plants. Check resources such as native plant and conservation groups.
- Protect and propagate rare plants and fungi.
- Be careful not to gather from polluted areas, including roadways, railways, industrial and agricultural runoff, sewage zones, oil spills, and places heavily sprayed with pesticides and/ or herbicides.

**Pattern Consciousness**
Don't harvest from the first patch you see. Go a bit further and spread out your collecting area, especially when collecting in a group.

**Everything Teaches**
- Lead by example. Let others know why you don't harvest certain plants or gather from specific areas.
- Help educate other gatherers whom you feel may be over harvesting.
- Let buyers know why you won't gather certain plants.

 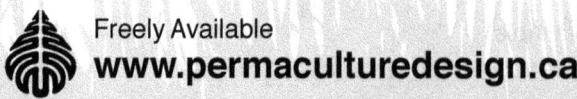

Freely Available
www.permaculturedesign.ca

**PERMACULTURE WORKSHEET**

# MEDICINE MAKING
## WILDCRAFTING PRINCIPLES

**Observe and Interact**
- Learn how to make accurate plant identification. It is important to know how to accurately identify plants to the species level.
- Go wildcrafting with someone more experienced your first few times.
- Map commonly visited areas by recording plant lists and locations for future visits and also to ensure that the landscape is regenerating rather than degenerating over time.

**Fair Share**
Be discreet when showing people wildcrafting locations. An area can easily be over harvested.

**Highest Use**
Rescue plants from areas that are going to be developed or destroyed. Besides gathering these plants as medicine, you can also help relocate the less common ones to similar habitats and gardens.

**Relocalize**
If you are harvesting plants for sale, gather and sell wildcrafted plants locally.
- Remember the take no more than 30% & leave 70% rule of thumb when harvesting.
- Consider growing and cultivating instead of wildcrafting.

**Long Term Planning**
Leave some of the strongest and most lush plants from an area you are wildcrafting. These are important to continue the local health and survival of a species.

**Respect Life**
- Be respectful of the plants you are gathering.
- Gathe thoughtfully and consciously.
- Give thanks for the harvest. In Native American traditions, tobacco or a strand of hair is left to show gratitude.

Freely Available
www.permaculturedesign.ca

# MEDICINE MAKING
## HARVESTING TIMES

Harvest times listed are the ideal times when the medicine will be at its prime. If everything is perfect, you will pay attention to where the plant is in its growth cycle and what phase the moon is in during harvest, preparation and storage.

Note that harvesting times have general patterns and may still vary based on the specific plant. It is recommended to research plants individually for specific details on harvesting practices.

In acute situations, medicine is medicine and harvest may fall outside of the optimum harvest time. The wildcrafting principles always apply.

**Seasonal Harvest**
Medicine often moves with the growth of the plant.
Roots are best harvested in when plants are in dormancy. Typically in the early spring or late fall.
If possible, allow perennial medicine to grow for 3 years before harvesting roots.

Leaf is best collected when the plant is in leaf. Typically throughout spring and summer and is dependent on the plant.

Flowers are best plucked when the plant is flowering

Seeds are best harvested when the plant is in seed, are dry and typically before frost. This may vary depending on the plant.

**Moon time Harvest**
Waning Moon
Energy is being drawn down, it is a good time to harvest roots.

New Moon
Energy is being drawn down, it is a good time to harvest roots.

Waxing Moon
Energy is being drawn up, so the most viable medicine is in the leaf and flower if in bloom.

Full Moon
Energy is at its highest, it is the best time to capture and store (bottle/ jar/ preserve, package).

Freely Available
www.permaculturedesign.ca

# MEDICINE MAKING
## HERBAL CLASSES

**Adaptogens :**
These herbs restore overall balance and strengthen the functioning of the body as a whole without impacting the balance of an individual organ or body system. Adaptogens can be stimulating and/or relaxing, many help improve focus, support immune system functioning, or provide some other broad-spectrum normalizing influence on unbalanced physiological processes.
A few adaptogenic herbs : Chaga, Holy Basil, Schisandra Berries, Ashwaghanda

**Alteratives :**
Alter slightly and correct conditions. They possess a tonic action without evacuation of the bowels.
A few Alterative herbs : Echinacea, Oregon Grape, Yellow Dock, Dandelion, Clover

**Anthelminitc :**
Aid in expelling stomach and intestinal worms.
A few Anthelmintic herbs : Wormwood, Garlic, Clove, Black Walnut

**Anti - inflammatory :**
Controls inflammation, a reaction to injury or infection.
A few Anti- inflammatory herbs : Devil's Club, St. John's Wort, Cayenne, Arnica

**Antispasmodic :**
Prevents and relieves spasms or convulsions.
A few Antispasmodic herbs : Peppermint, Passion Flower, Valerian, Catnip

**Astringent :**
Contracts tissues to diminish discharges of mucous or blood.
A few astringent herbs : Rose, Blackberry root and leaf, White Oak, Witch Hazel, Willow

**Carminitives :**
These herbs are often aromatic and help expel gas from the digestive system. This action can help ease bloating and gas related cramping.
A few carminative herbs : Fennel, Peppermint, Chamomile

Freely Available
www.permaculturedesign.ca

# MEDICINE MAKING
## HERBAL CLASSES

**Cholagogue :**
Stimulates flow of bile from the liver.
A few Cholagogue herbs : Dandelion, Milk Thistle, Peppermint, Burdock

**Demulcent :**
Sooth irritated mucous membranes. Service in common colds or coughs when taken internally and can be used as poultices for irritated skin.
A few demulcent herbs : Marshmallow Roots, Mullein (lungs), Cinnamon, Plantain

**Diaphoretic :**
Cause perspiration, but not as intensely as sudorifics. Mainly work directly on sweat glands when properly combined with other herbs. Great aid in releasing fever.
A few diaphoretic herbs : Ginger, Garlic, Cayenne, Elder, Yarrow

**Diuretic :**
Elimination helper. Promotes the secretion of urine. Mainly used for "lazy kidneys".
A few diuretic herbs : Dandelion, Juniper, Uva-Ursi, Cleavers

**Emmenagogue :**
Induces or hastens menstrual flow.
A few Emmenagogue herbs : Nettles, Mugwort, Feverfew, Yarrow

**Emolient :**
Mucilaginous herbs used as topical applications to help soothe, condition, and protect the skin.
A few emollient herbs : Aloe Vera, Comfrey, Marshmallow, Plantain

**Expectorant :**
Aid in decreasing and expelling excessive mucous that come with common colds, coughs, throat infection and bronchi irritation.
A few expectorant herbs : Elecampane, Mullein, Lobelia, Horehound

**Hemostatic :**
Controls the flow or stops the flow of blood
A few Hemostatic herbs : Yarrow, Calendula, Cattail

Freely Available
www.permaculturedesign.ca

# MEDICINE MAKING
## HERBAL CLASSES

**Hepatic :**
Acts on the liver.
A few Hepatic herbs : Danelion, Milk Thistle, Licorice, Turmeric

**Laxative :**
Stimulate secretion of the intestinal glands, creating a mild evacuation of softened stool.
A few Laxative herbs : Senna, Cascara Sagrada, Rhubarb, Chickweed

**Purgative:**
Promotes evacuation of the bowel.

**Nervine :**
Release stress, anxiety. Mildly sedative and can aid in sleep.
A few Nervine herbs : Chamomile, Valerian, Lemon Balm, Catnip, California Poppy

**Stimulant :**
Stimulates the central nervous system.
A few Stimulant herbs : Cayenne, Peppermint, Rosemary, Ginger

**Sudorific :**
Acts to increase perspiration
A few Sudorific herbs : Yarrow, Motherwort, Marjoram, Rosemary

**Stomachic :**
Aids the stomach and digestion action
A few Stomachic herbs : Mugwort, Rose Hips, Dandelion, Oregano

**Tonic :**
Tones and strengthens the entire system.
A few tonic herbs : Oat Tops, Nettle leaf, Dandelion, Milk Thistle Seed

Freely Available
www.permaculturedesign.ca

# MEDICINE MAKING
## PREPARATIONS

**MEDICINE MAKING MATERIALS LIST :**

This is a basic list of recommended and easily acquired materials to support in making most preparation.

- Baskets and paper bags for harvesting
- Glass / Pyrex Measuring cups on 1 cup, 2 cup and 4 cup sizes
- Metal strainer or Sieve
- Small pot
- Old blender, food processor or Vitamix
- Mason jars of all sizes
- Cheesecloth
- Masking Tape
- Permanent Marker
- Beeswax
- Olive Oil
- 100 proof Vodka
- Reusuable cloth rag for cleaning wax
- Tincture bottles, small glass jars with lids or other fun bottles for storing medicines.

Each plant that you work with has different methods of preparation. ALWAYS RESEARCH each plant individually to learn how it may be prepared. Here is a general list of some preparations, what they are and the farmer/ grandmother method for instructions.

**PREPARATIONS** :

Each plant that you work with has different methods of preparation. ALWAYS RESEARCH each plant individually to learn how it may be prepared. Here is a general list of some preparations, what they are and the farmer/ grandmother method for instructions.

Freely Available
www.permaculturedesign.ca

# MEDICINE MAKING
## PREPARATIONS

**DECOCTION :**
- Liquid preparation made by simmering plant matter with water
- Used when a plant is not soluble in boiling hot or cold water.
- Commonly used with:
  - Roots such as Licorice, Ginger, Oregon Grape or Dandelion
  - Polypore mushrooms like Artist Conk, Reishi and Chaga
  - Lichens
  - Branches like Seabuckthorn
- Decoctions extract the nutritional properties from the plant and are much gentler than tinctures

**Instructions :**
- Bring a pot of water to a boil
- Turn down to a simmer and add plant matter
- Use about 1-2 tsp for 1L of water
- Cover with lid
- Simmer for 5min - 5 hours or longer (depending on the plant).

**TEA INFUSION :**
- Steeped plant matter in either hot or cold water.
- Steeping is what allows the active ingredients to be extracted.
- Used on leafy/ light matter and flowers and plants containing volatile oils.
- Some examples would be Peppermint, Rose, Chamomile, Rosemary, Lavender
- Infusions extract the nutritional elements of the plant, and are much gentler than tinctures

**Instructions :**
- Bring water to a boil
- Turn water off
- Add 1- tsp of plant matter per cup of water to a vessel or tea strainer ( Best to use enamel, glass or porcelain if possible )
- Pour water over
- Cover and allow to sit 3- 10 min

*NEVER boil aromatic plants

Freely Available
www.permaculturedesign.ca

PERMACULTURE WORKSHEET 180

# MEDICINE MAKING
## PREPARATIONS

**SUSUN WEED'S NOURISHING HERBAL INFUSIONS**
- Strong liquid preparation for remineralizing and restoring the body
- Recommended infusions from Susun Weed are Netlles, Red Clover, Comfrey, Oats Straw and Linden and are taken once a week each. Other gentle plants like Raspberry Leaf, Yarrow, Dandelion and Hawthorn are good alternatives.
- It is not recommended to use plants with volatile oils like Peppermint, Lavender or Sage

Instructions :
- Bring water to a boil
- Turn water off
- Add 1 ounce of dried plant matter to a 1 litre mason jar
- Pour boiling water over top and seal
- Let sit for 4- 10 hours strain and refrigerate until fully consumed

**TONER:**
- Restores, tones and invigorates the skin.

**Instructions :**
- Make a strong infusion or decoction of a plant. Witches Hazel is commonly used.
- You will steep and simmer for longer than normal, usually about 8 hours for woody plants, research the plant to know how long to steep or simmer.
- Strain and store in the fridge, useable for 1 week.
- To preserve for extended use, you can cure with alcohol. Use half toner and half 40% ( 80 proof ) alcohol.

*For external use only

 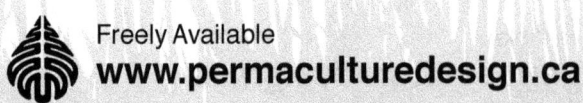

Freely Available
www.permaculturedesign.ca

**PERMACULTURE WORKSHEET 181**

# MEDICINE MAKING
## PREPARATIONS

### OIL INFUSION/ LINIMENT :
- Plant infused oil.
- Liniments may also be made using alcohol, glycerin or apple cider vinegar.
- Externally, often for massage or rubbing on skin
- Help with irritation, pain, swelling etc.
- Some can be taken internally for illness or preventative medicine.
- Some recommended plants for oil infusions are Comfrey, Usnea, Chamomile, Calendula, St. John's Wort.
- When taken internally, they are more gentle than tinctures and can typically be used more frequently.

### Instructions :
- Fill a jar with fresh plant matter
- To reduce water content at the start, you may dry plants for one day before infusing. Pluck flower petals off of the centre.
- Cover with oil or menstrum of choice.
- Olive oil is a good choice as it is a more neutral oil with less allergies. Almond oil is also commonly used.
- Seal the jar.
- Leave in a sunlit window for 1 week - 6 months ( Dependent on plant used. )
- Strain and let sit for one day.
- After sitting, water may pool at the bottom, strain again carefully and slowly until you see the water coming in and then discard the rest (mostly water).
- Store in a cool dry area to keep longer.

Freely Available
www.permaculturedesign.ca

# MEDICINE MAKING
## PREPARATIONS

**COMPRESS/ POULTICE :**
- Sometimes used to provoke the circulation of the blood or lymph in the body and may be applied either warm or hot.
- When applied cold they soothe pain and reduce swelling.
- Can also be used to clot blood and stop bleeding in deep wounds.
- Commonly used for:
  - Aches.
  - Colds.
  - Flu.
  - Pains.
  - Swellings.
  - Bites / stings.

**Instructions:**
- One or two heaping tablespoons of an herb or herbal combination are brought to boil in 1 cup of water
- Strain into a cup or pot
- Dip a 100% cotton pad, towel or sterile gauze in the strained liquid.
- Drain excess liquid
- Place cotton pad on the affected area while it is still warm.
- It is best covered with a piece of woolen material to trap the heat
- In acute situations, poultices can also be made by chewing up plant matter or mushing plant matter between fingers and compressing on affected area with hand.

Freely Available
www.permaculturedesign.ca

# MEDICINE MAKING
## PREPARATIONS

**OINTMENT / SALVE :**
- Therapeutic, fatty, soft substance for external application only.
- Typically has antiseptic, cosmetic or anti inflammatory properties.
- Not usually water soluble, however some ointments are composed of ingredients which are water soluble
- Typically used on the skin when the active principles of herbs are needed for longer periods of time which would then accelerate the healing process
- This may be in the case of:
  - Abrasion
  - Contusion
  - Injury
  - Burns
  - Muscle Spasms / Sprains / Strains

**Ingredients :**
- 3 parts Olive Oil or Oil infusion.
- 1 part grated beeswax
- Optional: essential oil
  (Approx. 3-5 drops per ounce. )

**Instructions :**
- Heat the beeswax on very low heat until melted, below 118 degrees and in a double boiler if possible.
- Mix in olive oil
- Pour into container and add 5- 7 drops essential oil(s) if desired. Do not mix.
- Seal and let cool
- Recommended Oils: Comfrey, Lavender, Tea Tree, Arnica, Wintergreen
- If the consistency is not to your desire, you can remelt and add beeswax to make it harder or oil to make it softer.

Freely Available
www.permaculturedesign.ca

PERMACULTURE WORKSHEET 184

# MEDICINE MAKING
## PREPARATIONS

**LOTION :**
- Water based, water soluble
- Used for rehydrating or rejuvenating the skin and for skin conditions
- Use olive oil and bees wax for a more natural approach

**Ingredients :**
- 6 parts olive oil ( or oil infusion. )
- 3 parts coconut oil
- 1 part beeswax in ounces
- 9 parts water at room temperature  (water is always equal to the oil mixture)
- Optiona l: essential oil ( approx 3-5 drops per ounce. )
- Optional : 1 tsp of borax for preservation

**Instructions :**
- in a pyrex measuring cup, add the beeswax, olive oil or oil infusion and coconut oil.
- Place in a pot with about 2 inches of water in it.
-  Heat the beeswax and oil mixutre on very low heat until melted, below
- Let cool  until you start to see a small amount of chunks in the mix.
- Pour into a blender or food processor.
- in another measuring cup add water and also add borax if desired. Make sure borax is mixed well and dissolved into the water mixture.
- Start mixing on low and slowly add water while mixing.
- Blend on high until you hear a sound change and then blend for another 5-7 min and until you see that the oils have emulsified with the water.  The mixture will turn white when this happens.
- Place into jars
- Refrigerate if possible for maximum preservation.
- A few recommended Oils: Calendula, Comfrey, Lavender, Borage, Arnica, Plantain.

Freely Available
www.permaculturedesign.ca

**PERMACULTURE WORKSHEET 185**

# MEDICINE MAKING
## PREPARATIONS

**TINCTURE :**
- Highly concentrated extract of medicinal properties of leaves, flowers, roots, seeds or bark
- Usually extracted with 100 proof alcohol or stronger.
- Tinctures are typically used in acute situations where healing is required immediately.
- Small amounts are taken and should be used with caution.
- It is recommended to use fresh plant matter whenever possible.

**Instructions :**
- Clean roots or plant matter in water (or brush off mushrooms )
- Finely chop plant matter and place into a tinted jar until it is almost full. Do not pack down.
- fill jar with 100 proof alcohol, make sure matter is covered and seal.
- If you must use dried plant matter, use 1 part plant matter to 5 parts alcohol.
- Let sit in a cool dark place for 4-6 weeks, shake often.
- Strain and place in dropper bottle for ingestion.

Instructions for double extracting polypore mushrooms:
- Fill an jar 2/3 rds full of finely chopped mushrooms
- Fill it to the top with 190 proof alcohol ( Everclear )
- Ensure matter is covered completely.
- Let this stand for 4- 6 weeks, shaking occasionally.
- Strain the mushrooms out of the alcohol and make a decoction with the matter ( Instructions above. )
- Combine 1 part of this tea with 1 part of the tincture.
- Transfer to a dropper bottle.
- Make sure to have a minimum 20% alcohol content.

Freely Available
www.permaculturedesign.ca

**PERMACULTURE WORKSHEET 186**

# MEDICINE MAKING
## PREPARATIONS

**FLOWER ESSENCE :**
- A light infusion of flowers, homeopathic
- Used typically for emotional healing

**Instructions :**
- On a sunny day, in the morning gently harvest flower petals from a desired plant that is in bloom. Fill a crystal bowl or a jar with spring water or distilled water and sprinkle the flower petals so that they are just covering the top of the water.
- Place in a sunny spot and let sit for 1 - 3 days (it must be sunny outside).
- The best time to do this is on or around a full moon.
- Strain and enjoy for about 1 week if kept refrigerated.
- To preserve for extended use, you can cure with alcohol. Use half essence and half 40% ( 80 proof ) alcohol.

**HONEY INFUSION**

- Honey infused with plant matter.
- Often used as a syrup alternative
- Offers both the healing properties of the plant and the honey.

**Instructions :**
- Fill a jar about half way with plant matter
- Warm a jar of honey to make it run more smoothly
- Cover the plant matter with the warm honey, seal and let sit for 1 week.
- Lightly warm the honey again and then strain.
- Enjoy!
- A few recommended herbs: Elderberry, Ginger, Borage, Lavender, Licorice Root, Marshmallow Root

Freely Available
www.permaculturedesign.ca

**PERMACULTURE WORKSHEET** 187

# MEDICINE MAKING
## HEALING PLANTS

### Borage - Borago Officinalis L.
Properties : Demulcent, Diaphoretic, Diuretic, Expectorant, Sedative.
Used for : depression, inflammation, fevers, chest and kidney problems, soothes damaged or irritated tissues, helps with skin and PMS. Seeds help to balance hormones.
Parts Used : Leaves, flower, seed
Harvest : When in leaf, flower and seed
Preparations : Infusion, tincture, liniment, lotion, poultice.
Contraindications : Do not prescribe for liver complaints or use with people who have weak liver.

### Calendula - Calendula Officinalis
Properties : Antispasmodic, Mild Laxative, Cholagogue, Diaphoretic
Used for : Fever, boils, abscesses, prevents vomiting, good for wounds, bruises, sprains, pulled muscles, sores and boils and all skin conditions. When taken internally, speeds up healing of wounds.
Parts Used : Leaves, Flowers.
Harvest : When in flower.
Preparations : Infusion, juice, tincture, salve, lotion.
Contraindications : None known.

### Chaga - Inonotus Obliquus
Properties: Adaptogen, Anti - inflammatory
Used for : Immune boosting, improves mental clarity, regulates the nervous system, anti viral, anti fungal, anti tumor, regulates digestion.
Parts Used : Mushroom
Harvest : Winter is the best time to harvest
Preparations : Decoction, tincture.
Contraindications : none known

### Chamomile - Matricaria recutita
Properties : Anti inflammatory; Antiseptic, Antispasmodic, Cholagogue; Diaphoretic, Nervine, Stomachic, Tonic.
Used for : Digestion, nervous tension, asthma, fevers, colds, burns, sunburns.
Parts Used : Flowers.
Harvest : When in flower.
Preparations : Tea, tincture, lotion, hair rinse.
Contraindications : Do not take if you have a hypersensitivity to ragweed pollens.

Freely Available
www.permaculturedesign.ca

# MEDICINE MAKING
## HEALING PLANTS

**Comfrey - Symphytum Officinale L. Aka. Knitbone**
Properties : Demulcent, Pectoral, Astringent
Used for : Eases pain and heals bruises, sprains, swellings and fractures. Very powerful in cough, ulcerated and inflamed lungs, hemorrhage, asthma and T.B., relieves sore stomach, sore bowels and kidney ulcers.
Parts Used : Roots, leaves.
Harvest : Leaves picked early summer before flowering and dried. Roots harvested during dormancy and dried or used fresh in liniment.
Preparations : Liniment, salve, syrup, decoction
Contraindications : Do not take internally for more than 4-6 weeks in the year. Consult a doctor before use during pregnancy. Do not apply to open wounds.

**Dandelion - Leontodon Taraxacum**
Properties : Cholagogue, Diuretic, Hepatic, Laxative, Stomachic, Tonic
Used for : Is helpful gall bladder and liver issues. Dandelion stimulates digestion and aids in jaundice, gall stones, constipation and urinary disorders, removes toxins from the body.
Parts Used : Flowers, leaves, stems, root
Harvest : Leaves year round, but best in early spring to early summer. Flowers in late spring and summer. Roots in early spring and mid to late fall.
Preparations : Leaves, flowers and stems used as an infusion, for food and compost tea. Roots used in decoctions and tinctures.
Contraindications : Not recommended for people with gallstones, heartburn or stomach ulcers.

**Blue Elder - Sambucus caerulea**
Properties : Analgesic; Antiseptic; Astringent; Diaphoretic; Febrifuge; Haemostatic; Laxative; Stomachic; Tonic.
Used for : Colds, fevers, blood poisoning, stomach problems, burns, sprains, bruises and antiseptic for itches and open sores, sometimes used as an eyewash.
Parts Used: Flowers, berries, root, bark
Harvest : Leaves year round, but best in early spring to early summer. Flowers in late spring and summer. Roots in early spring and mid to late fall.
Preparations : Tea, syrup, wash, ointment
Contraindications : some sources recommend that it is not used during pregnancy or lactation.

Freely Available
www.permaculturedesign.ca

# MEDICINE MAKING
## HEALING PLANTS

**Oregon Grape - Mahonia Aquafolium**
Properties : Alterative, Hepatic, Antitumor, Diuretic, Tonic Laxative, Tonic.
Used for : Traditionally the roots are used to treat loss of appetite and debility,also treats psoriasis and eczema syphilis, hemorrhages, stomach complaints, impure blood conditions, sore throats gastritis and general digestive weakness. It stimulates the kidney and gallbladder and acts as a laxative.
Harves t: Roots and root bark collected in late autumn and early spring then dried or used fresh in tincture.
Parts Used : Roots / Rhizome, Flowers, Fruit
Preparations :  Roots as a tincture, decoction and a rinse for sore throat. Fruit may be eaten as well as flowers .
Contraindications : Oregon grape should not be used when chronic gastrointestinal irritation or inflammation is present, such as irritable bowel

**Peppermint - Mentha X Piperita L.**
Properties : Stimulant, Stomachic, Sudorific, Antispasmodic, Nervine.
Use for : Stomach,  headache, flatulence, colic, dizziness, fever, measles and convulsions. Smell to increase energy and focus.
Parts Used : Whole herb.
Harvest : Cut whole plant before flowering, or use leaves during whole growing season.
Preparations : Infusion.
Contraindications : *NEVER BOIL*

**Plantain - Plantago Major L.**
Properties : Cooling, Alterative, Emollient, Diuretic
Used for : poisonous bites and stings, good externally for boils, tumors, inflammation. Roots and leaves influence glandular system, helps with scanty urine and aching in the lumbar due to kidney and bladder trouble.
Parts Used : Herb, Root.
Harvest : Cut plant throughout growing season, used fresh, juiced or dried.
Preparations : Poultice, Salve, Infusion, Syrup
Contraindications : None known.

Freely Available
www.permaculturedesign.ca

# MEDICINE MAKING
## HEALING PLANTS

### Red Raspberry - Rubus Idaeus
Properties: Astringent, Tonic, Stimulant, Alterative
Used for : Gargle with it to remove cankers, sore throat and spongy gums, relieves nausea, diarrhea, helps during labour and with after pains. Use as an eye wash for opthalmia.
Parts Used : Leaf, Berry.
Harvest : Leaves picked young, before flowering, berries when ripe.
Preparations: Infusion of leaf, berries eaten raw or cooked.
Contraindications: None known.

### Red Belted Polypore - Fomitopsis pinicola
Properties : Adaptogen, Analgesic, Anti diarrhea, Anticancer, Diaphoretic, Digestive.
Parts Used : Young flesh.
Used for : treatment of headache, diarrhea, cancer, fever, jaundice and irritable bowel syndrome, excessive urination. Also acts as a tonic to reduce inflammation of the digestive tract. The Cree Indians used it like a styptic pencil to stop the bleeding in cuts.
Harvest : Year round.
Preparations: Decoctions and tinctures.
Contraindications: Can turn hair grey with extended use.

### Rosemary - Rosmarinus officinalis - L.
Properties : Antiseptic, Antispasmodic, Aromatic, Astringent, Cholagogue, Diaphoretic, Emmenagogue. Nervine, Ophthalmic, Stimulant, Tonic.
Used for:  Depression, increases energy, headaches, cholic, colds, nervous issues, headaches, rheumatism, blood pressure and lack of appetite.  Can be used in the treatment of toxic shock syndrome.
Parts Used : Leaves, Flower.
Harvest: When in leaf or flower.
Preparations : Dried, essence, steam, essential oil.
Contraindications : Some people may be allergic.

Freely Available
www.permaculturedesign.ca

# MEDICINE MAKING
## HEALING PLANTS

### Shaggy Old Mans Beard - Usnea hirta
Properties: Antibacterial, Anti fungal, Antiviral, Antimicrobial.
Parts Used: Whole lichen.
Used for : treatment of colds, cough, menstrual cramps, candida, arthritis, rheumatism, gout, sciatica. Immune boosting.
Harvest: Harvest in late spring. For most ethical harvest, find fresh fallen branches after a storm with fresh Usnea. Gather from a clean location as it can absorb heavy metals.
Preparations: Use as a liniment ( Most effective ), tincture, decoction and salves.
Contraindications : Overuse of Usnea for colds, flu and infection can damage spleen.

### Valerian - Valeriana Officinalis L.
Properties: Antispasmodic, Stimulant, Hypnotic, Nervine, Tonic.
Used for : Sleep, nervous tension, cramping and lowering blood pressure. Helps with painful menstruation, cramps, hypertension and IBS.
Parts Used : Root/ Rhizome.
Harvest :  Root harvested in second year of growth, after leaves have died down.
Preparations : Cold infusion, tincture, compost tea.
Contraindications : Prolonged use can lead to addiction.
*NEVER BOIL*

### Yarrow - Achillea Millefolium L.
Properties: Diaphoretic, Diuretic, Stimulant, Astringent, Tonic and Alterative.
Used for : Raising body temperature and equalizes circulation, producing perspiration. Relieves fever, colds, typhoid fever, dysentry, blood hemorrhages and inflammation of the bladder.
Parts Used: Flowering Herb.
Harvest: Cut when in flower and dry.
Preparations: Infusion, poultice/ compress.
Contraindications: Some people experience hyper sensitivity to Yarrow.

### Witch Hazel - Hamamelis virginiana - L.
Properties: Astringent, Sedative, Tonic.
Helpful with bruises, varicose veins, sore muscles, haemorrhoids, diarrhea, dysentry, internal bleeding, prolapsed organs and eye inflammation.
Parts Used: Seed, bark, branches.
Harvest: Just after flowering.
Preparations: Eye drops, tonics.

Freely Available
www.permaculturedesign.ca

# MEDICINE MAKING
## RESOURCES

Food and Medicine Plants of the Coastal First Peoples - Nancy Turner
Foraging and Feasting - Dina Falconi
Healthy Bodies, Heavenly Hair - Dina Falconi
Planting the Future - Saving Our Medicinal Herbs
Healing Wise - Susun Weed
Herbal Recipes for Vibrant Health - Rosemary Gladstar
The Complete Herbs Sourcebook - David Hoffman
Fungal Pharmacy - Robert Rogers
Boreal Herbal - Beverley Gray
Harmonic Arts - Yarrow Willard - www.harmonicarts.ca
Plants for a Future - www.pfaf.org
Dominion Herbal College - www.dominionherbal.com
Rosemary Gladstar www.sagemountain.com
Dina Falconi www.botanicalartspress.com
Susun Weed www.susunweed.com

"There's wisdom in the old adage let food be thy medicine and medicine by thy food. Truly, it's the diet and lifestyle choices we make on a daily basis that most affect our long - term health and well - being. It's odd that health care becomes an issue only when health is absent and medicine is deemed effective only if it is so potent that the possible side effects are often as serious as the initial diagnosis. Health care really makes more sense if we care enough about our health to attend to it on a regular basis, and medicine makes more sense if it is strong enough to be effective but still kind to our bodies. Always start with the most effective but least harmful remedy. Isn't the healers primary creed first do no harm?"
- **Rosemary Gladstar** www.sagemountain.com

**Source Curriculum:** Dina Falconi, Dominion Herbal College, Robert Rogers, Rosemary Gladstar, Susun Weed, David Hoffman, Barbara Cotgrave
**Envoy:** Delvin Solkinson www.visionarypermaculture.com
**Foundational Work :** Kym Chi www.gigglingchitree.com
**Design :** Sijay James www.onbeyondmetamedia.com

Freely Available
www.permaculturedesign.ca

**PERMACULTURE WORKSHEET 193**

# DESIGN FUTURES
## NEXT LEVEL EDUCATION

"*Permaculture education is providing a model by having no boundaries and enabling fields of study to splinter off according to interest, potential and need. Examples include the ecovillage network as well as school gardens which fly off from permaculture, floating away like lovely little sections of seeds which can start germinating elsewhere. Instead of turning us all into brain surgeons, accountants or carpenters, permaculture can produce a diversity of people who go out into society to enrich it. Permaculture people can be of any age or gender because everyone is equally capable of absorbing the materials. It's an open system with no boundaries, no leader, and no board of education. We are getting back to people centered education. Permaculture seeks to provide people with good, relevant knowledge that they can act on the directive from E. F. Schumacher who said 'The best gift you can give people is relevant information and knowledge'.*"
- Rosemary Morrow

Endless gratitude to everyone who has explored and made us of this book. As part of my life work, it brings me great joy that it can be shared. As a free, open source resource it's my hope that those who are inspired will take the time to share this both as a digital file and printed pages with anyone who may benefit from it. You can find promotional text and graphics for sharing here
**www.dewpermaculture.com/core-curriculum-notes.**

Teachers are encouraged to upgrade their curriculum with these notes and may choose to share individual pages as worksheet handouts. Students, designers and consultants may use these notes as a 'Designers Checklist' to expand their approach to learing and applying permaculture in different contexts.

Those wanting to further support this work can purchase hardcopy versions direct from the on-demand printer at Lulu. Make sure to look for the discount code as Lulu always has a sale on. **www.lulu.com/shop/gaiacraft-and-delvin-solkinson/gaiacraft-permaculture-design-core-curriculum-notes/hardcover/product-23314805.html**

Donations towards this project, the development of other language editons, and to the ongoign design of other free open sources permaculture learning and teaching tools can be made with **paypal to delvin@crystalandspore.com**

May any merit generated by this work be dedicated to the benefit of all beings.
*Delvin Solkinson, Winte Solstice 2017*

Freely Available
**www.permaculturedesign.ca**

# PERMACULTURE DESIGN NOTES
## REVIEWS AND SUPPORT

This carefully curated collection from Delvin Solkinson's 15 year journey is a wonderful reference that will prove to be the perennial words of positive works everywhere.
- **Larry Santoyo, Permaculture Academy** www.permacultureacademy.com

This is a foundational work that will inform and guide many into the future. I am deeply inspired and grateful for the immensely valuable contribution of the Permaculture Design Core Curriculum Notes. Everyone interested in learning, teaching and facilitating Permaculture will benefit from this very practical and beautifully crafted text. It skillfully weaves together essence, depth of content and the 'Fair Share' ethic. It researches and brings forward wisdom and teachings from the past, flavours it with present brilliance and developments and offers a foundation for the next evolution of Permaculture.
- **Robin Clayfield** www.dynamicgroups.com.au

Amazing energy and input. This is a gift to Permaculture.
- **Looby Macnamara** www.loobymacnamara.com

This is a dense but well formatted book offers many strategies and techniques to teachers, designers and practitioners. Delvin and the team have summarized most the knowledge we hold in permaculture. The summaries collate all material and information used by most teachers. I could see Delvin's encyclopaedic mind through it all. The team deserves a huge 'thank you' for pulling all this together. It works best through its checklists and summaries. This book gives abundantly and freely to all people - permaculturists or not.
- **Rosemary Morrow** www.bluemountainspermacultureinstitute.com.au

Permaculture offers a set of tools to design sustainable lifestyles and with this book, Permaculture Design Core Notes, Delvin Solkinson and Kym Chi have brought together the many elements that creates this integral whole system. The Foundational Concepts offer the reader a window into building blocks of Permaculture. As the book evolves, a Permaculture curriculum unfolds offering a guide to anyone who wants to practice and/or share the knowledge of this effective system in any environment- from teaching children to adults to direct application on the land and in community. This is a book of succinct and contemplative lists and critical thinking questions providing ideas to springboard the reader to further research and application.
- **Jude Hobbs Cascadia Permaculture** www.cascadiapermaculture.com

Freely Available
www.permaculturedesign.ca

**PERMACULTURE WORKSHEET** 195

# PERMACULTURE DESIGN NOTES
## REVIEWS AND SUPPORT

"A wonderful effort and full of great information."
- **Max Lindegger**
www.ecologicalsolutions.com.au

"The book provides a useful summary for teachers and students of permaculture alike. It is well designed, thought provoking, and clear. I am going to be leafing through this potent, comprehensive collection for some time."
- **Maddy Harland, Editor & Co-Founder of Permaculture Magazine**
www.permaculturemag.org

Scope and Depth.
All projects, be they land or life require both to be successful. In an international pilgrimage to permaculture pioneers, practitioners and projects Delvin Solkinson has deftly crafted this tome sourcing from over two dozen living pillars of wisdom. For craftsmen, seeking high grade tools to progress their work in regenerative living, I recommend this book. My sincere gratitude to Delvin for his work.
- **Javan K. Bernakevitch**
www.allpointsdesign.ca

Permaculture Design Core Curriculum Notes provides permaculture teachers, students, and practitioners with a holistic outline for permaculture literacy. This book deserves a place on your bookshelf next to Bill Mollison's Permaculture: A Designers' Manual.
- **Scott Mann**
www.thepermaculturepodcast.com

The Core Curriculum Notes are way more than just an outline of the Permaculture Design Course curriculum. They are an index to a whole process, from the culture of a class and presence of an instructor, to a road map of where students can go beyond the PDC. It's always fascinating to see how someone as deeply studied as Delvin arranges and sequences the curriculum, borne of his own trial and error and the trials and errors of his mentors and teachers. I will definitely be referencing this text as I do my own work, and am very appreciative that this is put together as an open source document to lift up all teachers in the Permaculture field.
- **Andrew Millison**
www.permaculturerising.com

Freely Available
www.permaculturedesign.ca

**PERMACULTURE WORKSHEET 196**

www.ingramcontent.com/pod-product-compliance
Lightning Source LLC
Chambersburg PA
CBHW080245170426
43192CB00014BA/2570